The OTHER SIDE
of the
Struggle

Supporting a Spouse Who Struggles with Mental Illness

Danielle Foisy

Danielle Foisy

5 Fold Media
Visit us at www.5foldmedia.com

This book is dedicated to my Grandma Jan. She herself lived with a spouse with mental illness. Thank you for showing me what unconditional love and unwavering commitment looks like. Thank you for modeling what a follower of Jesus Christ looks like and always believing in me.

I want to also thank my husband for being courageous enough to allow me to share our story and allow our story to help others and bring glory to God. I am so blessed to be able to walk this life with you. I love you.

Contents

Foreword

D epression and other mood disorders have become very common. There are many resources to help the one suffering, but very few resources to help the spouse who is usually bewildered and feeling helpless. This book fills that gap and has been written specifically to help a spouse navigate what is likely the darkest time in their marriage.

Ms. Foisy describes in detail what she and her husband went through and then the wonderful victory that they achieved through a combination of faith, medication, and counseling. This book is all about hope and the steps that God showed them to get there. I would recommend it to any couple who is facing the mountain of mental illness. You will get the tools you need to be victorious.

Grant Mullen M.D.
Author of *Emotionally Free*

Introduction

Mental Illness is something that is not talked about a lot in the church; it is actually secreted in many circumstances because of the shame, stigma, and even embarrassment that comes with admitting the struggle your family is going through. My goal is to change that, to start a movement that we start the conversation and start talking about mental illness within churches and Christian circles. We need to be open, especially in the church; we need to bring it into the light and not allow it to fester in the darkness where the enemy has power.

This book is about overcoming trials and storms through God's strength. It is about what it looks like supporting a spouse, family member, or someone close to you through dark times of mental illness, depression, or addiction. It is an attempt to blend Christian views and worldly views together to understand more about mental illness from the struggling person's point of view and also to look at ways to be on the other side of that struggle.

The stigma around mental illness is prominent in both non-Christian and Christian circles, but surprisingly the secular world is actually better at accepting these struggles than the church is. This needs to change; just because we are Christians does not mean we are freed from the difficulties of this fallen world. The difference is that we have Jesus Christ to help us through those times.

There is a misconception that if someone is struggling it is because they have sinned and therefore they are not able to live a good life and are a lost cause. Another misconception is that as a Christian you can only deal with problems from the spiritual sense and that you struggle because you are weak and/or possessed. Please hear what I am saying.

The Other Side of the Struggle

Prayer and the divine intervention from God are necessary—I will never discredit that as part of the solution—but when dealing with something serious such as mental illness, in my opinion, it is not wrong to open the situation to additional natural solutions as well.

There is a lot of push back from the Christian world about the validity of mental illness; some say every illness is a spiritual problem, claiming it is because of demonic possession. But we need to be careful not to over-spiritualize the situation. We live here on earth, and until we are living in eternity we will continuously come up against the ways of the world; some of the world's ways are not bad but complement the work you are doing on the spiritual side of the problem. I am not saying there is not a spiritual aspect to mental illness; I truly believe there is because we live in a fallen world with sin everywhere and in everything. What I am saying from experience is that in some situations, not trying to find a solution on top of prayer and spiritual solutions can limit the progress of someone struggling.

Stating that someone struggles because of something they have done is kicking them when they are already down and hurting, which truly can be disheartening to someone who is struggling and is an enormous reason why people do not talk about their struggles in the church. There is shame and fear attached to the struggle when you are Christian because to admit the struggle can be twisted into saying that you are a bad person and not close to God.

On the flip side, the worldly view says that mental illness is only based on a chemical imbalance in the brain, that it is something completely beyond your control and that the only solution is to be medicated for the rest of your life. My goal is to blend both these views together; there is an element of medicine and psychology to it, but there is also a spiritual battle going on as well, and I believe there is a mixture of both that can create an environment for success.

Even when I am talking about the worldly solution for mental illness, I believe God works through those methods, so I don't believe that using what Christians would deem "worldly" solutions excludes God from the equation. God always has a plan and a purpose, but many people do not believe that their mental illness can be something that was done on purpose and can be part of God's plan. God uses our suffering and our pain, our shortcomings and our defects for His glory; so next time you become frustrated at the life you have been handed, remember that God allowed this to be your reality. And once you stop fighting it you can start to learn what His plan is for it and the glory can be revealed.

As I have walked this journey into the world of mental illness, I have come across a wonderful Christian mental illness doctor who I feel sums it up perfectly. Dr. Grant Mullen says that mental illness is simply when you have thoughts you don't want and can't stop thinking them. How you think is medical; what you think is spiritual. Dr. Mullen compares medication for mental illness to be the same as using eyeglasses when your eyes cannot see properly. You would never be expected to just "push through it" and try and see better, and Dr. Mullen's point on mental illness is just the same. If there is a medication that can help control your thoughts, you can then be freed to think about what you want. This really shows how the medical—or worldly—side of things does not have to be opposite or contradict the spiritual side of things; they can actually complement each other.[1]

In my personal situation, it is my spouse who dealt with mental illness, but many people have parents, siblings, cousins, aunts or uncles, or even close friends who struggle with these things. My perspective may sometimes focus in on the spousal relationship, but my hope is that you can take away the same concepts no matter the relationship.

I also want to express that even if someone is struggling in the deepest and darkest of ways, it is never acceptable or okay to allow abusive behavior to continue. I am not an expert in this area; this is my own experience and learning within the world of mental illness, so please do not take anything I say in this book as a professional guideline or psychological advice.

Being in a relationship, especially a marriage, to someone who is battling something completely separate from anything to do with you is

---

1. Dr. Grant Mullen, *Emotionally Free*, 2nd ed. (Tate Pub & Enterprises llc., 2013).

so unbelievably difficult. You are helpless; nothing you do can help or change things, and it's a very weird place to be. No one really understands it or your situation and you will probably get all sorts of advice that can tangle your brain even more. People want to support you but they don't know what to say, what is wrong to say, or how to problem solve it, but they are usually just trying to help. You need to know that the people who want to help are how you will survive, so I urge you not to push them away because they don't understand what you are going through. It's hard because you are so close to the situation and you see every intricate detail of it—they don't. Keep reminding yourself of it because it's very easy to lose sight of that truth.

Sometimes it feels like you are being tossed around by an ocean storm; waves keep coming and you don't even have time to recover from one crashing wave before another comes and takes you out again. It feels very out of control and overpowering. This is a metaphor to help describe the chaos that comes with someone in your life who is struggling with mental illness. There are moments it is unfair to you, very unfair. You may be doing everything—taking care of the house, the kids, and working—you are doing it all, and it is unfair. But that is life, and life is not fair, and your attitude in it all determines where you go with that unfairness. Your behavior, your words, and your actions all count toward how your story ends; keep that in mind if you are in the midst of this scenario.

I have heard several times that in marriage, when one is down, the other is up. When one is weak, the other is strong. That may be true for the most part, but it is not always the case. There are many exceptions to that rule, but if you don't know that you may be setting up unrealistic expectations for your marriage. Mental illness is definitely one of the exceptions to that rule. In the past, if I was down, it didn't always mean that my husband would be in a good enough head space to pick me back up. I know that doesn't sound fair, and sometimes it's not. But as I mentioned already, life and marriage don't always come with complete fairness.

On a deeper level, this book is about the battle, the war we are in. It is not against your spouse, friends, or co-workers; it is the unseen war we are all in, whether we want to be or not, whether we see it or not. The enemy is real—he is a warrior of darkness and has ample amounts of ammunition to use against us. The worst part is he is sneaky, deceitful, and able to mask all his efforts from us while he is using them against us. The only weapon we can use to save ourselves in this battle is God.

I want to allow you the opportunity to get to know me and my story about our battle with mental illness and the journey we have gone through before we go into ways to deal with it. I want to introduce you to a concept that I will talk about many times in the book: "Spirals." As my husband struggles with mental illness, he would have what I have called "spirals" or what others would call "episodes." A spiral is where something would trigger him and send him into a downward spiral of negativity, irrational thoughts, and believing all the lies Satan was whispering in his ears. I would never know how many hours or days they were going to last, but there was no way to get him out of them either.

In December 2016, our world was falling apart. We had just moved across the country from one side of Canada to the other with our two little girls, who were one and three years old at the time. Little did we know that God had planned a year of breaking us down to our rawest form of selves to start re-building us into His masterpieces.

For the eight years I have known my husband, he has struggled with a mental illness that was undiagnosed and untreated, yet he has been struggling himself for over twenty years. He was adamantly against using medication and going to doctors when I came into the picture because he had tried them and they sadly did not help or work for him. We had been living in the Rocky Mountains for six years before moving. My husband's biggest passion in life is rock climbing, but what we did not know at the time was the mountains were his escape, his coping mechanism. We had just moved into the middle of a city, so now he had no escape. After we moved we knew it was bad but we were "coping." (I say that mildly—we were actually drowning.)

The Other Side of the Struggle

This big change combined with the loss of his coping mechanisms in the mountains were a recipe for a disaster—and that is exactly what we got. In 2016, our storm exploded; things got very dark. My husband was spiraling out of control and just didn't have it in him to save himself. After months and months of the situation escalating, something had to be done. One Saturday night he was in one of the worst spirals we ever experienced and he made a suicidal threat that he was going to burn our house down with himself in it. I didn't honestly believe he was going to do anything because he had never gotten close to hurting himself, and especially not me or the kids, but I had never seen my husband this low and it was getting to the point where I felt like I didn't know this person anymore. After talking with our pastor and close friends of his who know him extremely well, we all decided that something drastic needed to be done; we could not continue like this for the well-being of our family. I made the decision to call the police—by far one of the hardest decisions of my life—hoping to get my husband some help. The point of calling was for them to take him to the hospital so he could get a proper psychiatric assessment. We could not go on any further not knowing what we were dealing with; it was overtaking every aspect of our lives, and I had two little girls to think about above myself.

Unfortunately, things got even messier before they got better. My husband saw the police and panicked, deciding to run away. It took forty-eight hours for them to find him; I cannot even begin to tell you what those forty-eight hours looked like for me, but it was sickening. According to our laws, if they found him after forty-eight hours and he looked fine, they were no longer allowed to do anything. Because it had been over forty-eight hours after they found him in his home town, they were not able to apprehend him because he appeared to be mentally "stable." So after they talked with him and deemed him "levelheaded," they left. So after all of the craziness, all that was accomplished was I called the police on my husband and now there was nothing they could do.

I was devastated, and obviously my husband was more than upset with me, but on top of that nothing was accomplished for his mental state. I tried to talk with him, but he was still in a bad spiral so the conversation was pointless in my opinion. During that conversation I got a phone call from the police. They were also not happy with how things ended up and said they had found a loophole to try and get him the help he needed. They decided they were going to charge him for the type of suicidal threat he made because he made it against property. Their hope was that he would have to see a judge who could order him to get a psychiatric assessment. That, of course, was not good news to hear for any of us; I was very distraught because I was trying to get my husband help, not get him in trouble with the police. With this new development he ran off into the night again, starting another twenty-four-hour period of not knowing where he was and if he was okay. To this day, I am not sure what triggered him to come back to his senses and call me, but he eventually did, saying he had to stop running and needed to "face the music" so to speak. He came back to the town we were living in and sat in a jail cell for the morning.

Prior to this experience, my husband had never spoken to a police officer in his life, so this was new territory for both him and us. That morning he sat in a jail cell was a new rock bottom for him, a place he needed to get to as we look back now. They ended up releasing him but he got a court date and left with the understanding that he still had to deal with the repercussions of what had happened. Because there was a court date, he agreed to see a doctor to make it look like he was trying to get better. He truly had no intention of listening to the doctor but went anyway because it would look good to the courts. Looking back, I see why such drastic methods had to be taken; we would have likely "coasted" for the rest of our lives if there was not something pressing him to seek out help. Thankfully, the doctor we had was involved with a great three-part program for people struggling with mental illness. The first part was professional counseling, the second part was a thorough psychiatric assessment, and third was medication and finding resources in the area to seek out. When he was first prescribed the medication he would not take it, but he did participate in the counseling part of the program. It took over a month for him to even come around to trying the medication, which I attribute to the fact that during that time I spent every spare second on my knees in my prayer room.

The Other Side of the Struggle

I want to show you the journey we went through to overcome a giant obstacle that Satan designed to try to tear us down and how God victoriously performed miracle after miracle to save us from it. I want to allow you to see both sides of it—from my husband's perspective as the struggler and mine as a wife to him in this situation from the other side of the struggle.

Husband:

I like to use the analogy of an avalanche to help bring the metaphor to life. You see, an avalanche occurs when its weight exceeds its strength. That happens to us sometimes when the weight of our issues becomes too much for us to carry and we start to slide uncontrollably, unable to stop ourselves or the destruction it's creating along its path. It accelerates rapidly and grows in volume as more gets added to it and less gets done to stop it. Metaphorically speaking, the action of being pummeled by an avalanche is like being beaten by the enemy, suffocated by his lies and held captive by his chains of failure and defeat. I lived for over a decade of my life with an untreated, undiagnosed mental illness that I refused to deal with. I was hurting myself and my family and had surrendered to the darkness as if that's all there was for me on this earth. We had very young children at the time, and I knew that although they might not understand now, they would one day; but I just couldn't snap out of it. With mental illness, it is just not that easy to break free. With enough distractions I managed to get by, but the move away from the mountains really triggered the biggest downward spiral I had ever experienced. After moving, I sank into a pretty dark place, darker than I had ever gone, and just could not find a way to get myself out of it. Over time, it just kept getting worse and worse until finally it just exploded.

Danielle:

From my side of the events, it was an emotional rollercoaster. Fear and worry were the main struggles at the beginning. After those feelings, hopelessness and despair came on. I was literally watching my husband drown but was terrified to lose him completely if I stepped in and tried to help. What I learned in this process is what complete dependence on God truly is. He brought me to a place where the world could no longer help me and I had to hold on to His rope for dear life if I was going to get by. In an attempt to do this, the only solution I came up with was to get down on my knees and pray. I ended up making a little prayer room in our basement and took it all to Him there. Many people prayed with me during that time, and it was amazing to see what God started to do when we started to surrender our lives to Him and for me to really give my husband over to God. This situation made me risk my security and surrender the life we were living over to God so He could work the mess out of it. In hindsight I can see now what God was doing, but in the midst of the hardest moments it was very difficult to see or feel any hope. At one point, God spoke into my heart and said, "Look at this mess; this is what happens when you try and do it. Now watch Me work." Within days of that moment our lives started to change forever; my husband walked through the door after all this prayer and said to me, "I'm done living like this; I'm willing to try the medication." I will never forget that day or that moment! I give all the glory to God for finally getting us to the moment when we were going to start climbing out of the darkness rather than being overtaken by it.

Husband:

I was finally able to get to a broken enough place, a rock-bottom kind of place, to allow God to start working. He stripped me down to the rawest form of who I am and started tearing away the junk—the lies, the deceit, the strongholds, the pain, the injustice—and started replacing it with His love, grace, forgiveness, and healing. God restored me from this suffering, like putting me through a refining fire so I could be given the chance to be who He created me to be, but I wasn't going to get there with everything I was holding on to. He opened the door to worldly help that I needed within the medical and psychological world.

Danielle:

I feel like this whole process has brought me into a much deeper and intimate relationship with God. In that happening, He has revealed more steps in the plan He has for my life and our life as a family. In the early weeks of my husband's hike up and out of the mountain of darkness, I felt strongly that God was asking me to start giving things up and following Him instead. Even though we had just gone through one of the most traumatic experiences as a family, I decided to obey that request and ended up leaving the secular career that I was in at the time.

Husband:

I finally got myself the medical help I needed in order to be able to clearly see what was happening to my life. I got a proper diagnosis from professionals and got onto the right medication that thankfully was one that has been working and gave me mental clarity that I had never experienced before. Getting out of that deep darkness has allowed me to see things so much clearer, and I have been able to make many positive changes because of that. It's hard to believe I was living in that darkness for so long. As I have started to recover from this, I have started restoring my relationship with God. As I have done that, and as we as a family has started to walk in the obedience of God's will, doors have begun to fly open. God also rectified the situation and the court case was completely dropped when they saw the progress I was making.

I was so against getting help, taking medication, and admitting that I couldn't do it on my own, and I know I am not the only one sitting in that place in life. I know God had me live this out so I can take the experience and help others, teaching and giving others the courage and strength to get out of the darkness the enemy is keeping them captive in. I believed the lies of the enemy for years; they consumed all my thoughts, and I would have lost everything if I kept down that path. I know the enemy is attacking people all over the world with the same tactics. So if our testimony, our story, and our words can help just one person then it will all be worth it.

Danielle:

This is just one battle we've experienced. God restored and redeemed each of us personally, our relationships with Him, and our marriage. We believe He has given us this experience so we can help others. When I was enduring this battle, there were not very many resources for me as a spouse of someone who is struggling, and that is how we got here today. No one needs to go through these experiences alone and with nowhere to turn for support.

I want to shed some light on what the year looked like after the storm exploded. We got the professional intervention we needed. I know that medication is a touchy subject, especially in the Christian world. There are a lot of opinions about it, a lot of research and debate about whether it is the right choice. I can only say that this particular choice has to come from within your own family. We battled long and hard without it and got to the point where we were willing to try it, and in just days we both were starting to see something positive. We directly credit God for this miracle even though we used the intervention of medication; the timing, swiftness, and all the miracles surrounding the entire situation proved undeniably that divine intervention from God was involved.

Someone said to me once that if my husband had a medical sickness such as diabetes, we would not think twice about using medication. We were at the point where we had tried other ways and could not get over this hump of darkness and decided to go the medical route. For our specific situation, using the medication helped things to start becoming "controllable." Our marriage had suffered in this state of "coasting" until the next storm came for years; for my husband it was over a decade. For the first time in what seemed like forever, there was a clarity and an understanding of what we were dealing with—something that changes things drastically in a situation like this. Not only did God guide us into the professional and medical help that was needed, He was taking care of us mentally, emotionally, physically, and geographically too. We got an opportunity to move to a town that was much more suited for our lifestyle and happiness. This opportunity not only gave us work but also wonderful community and church. God picked this specific community because there were other areas of the past that needed to be dealt with in my husband's heart.

It was a whirlwind of a year, and even though there were some extremely dark moments, I wouldn't change it to be where we are now. I can truly say I have a new husband and that God performed countless miracles. On the one-year anniversary of the day our old life exploded, both of us were now working in the field of our passions. I am writing and working in missions, which is my passion, and my husband started an adventure business to pursue his passions. It is really extraordinary that in one year's time so much of the darkness that took over a decade to build could be healed. That is the power of Jesus—that is the power of what the Holy Spirit can do.

This is the story of the hardest experience our little family has ever gone through. I can truly say that God uses everything for His good—every single tear and every single broken heart. I can genuinely say that God held me in every scary and dark moment and that He honored every moment I ran to Him. We have overcome a very ugly time and our hearts are hungry for God more than ever. I trust His will for my life and I will happily walk in His obedience because I know that is where I belong. I also want to be very real and truthful; this is not a fairytale story but real life. Mental illness is not a virus that comes and eventually goes. We still deal with side effects of mental illness all the time, but what this experience has taught us is that there are ways to cope, ways to handle it when it comes up, and how to identify triggers and prevent unnecessary spirals from taking us down. It has also given us a promise that God was victorious then and will be every single time in the future, even if there are aspects of this we deal with again.

God healed so many hearts by our situation; He has brought so many people in our family and close friends back into relationship with Him, and what we went through and came out on the other side of had a ripple effect to many people. In the big picture, our family is doing great. We still have normal life experiences, of course—we still have bad days, our kids are crazy some (most) days, and we have normal marital issues. I am not saying things are perfect. But things are controllable and better than they ever have been. God has saved my husband from something that could have destroyed him; He saved our family from continuing to drown in the enemy's plan. He saved us, protected us, guided us, and pulled us out of darkness and into His light because that is who He is!

Don't ever forget what His character is when you are in the middle of a storm—it is hard to see and feel, but His truth never changes. If there is anything you can get from reading this book, I hope that is what you take. I also want to be very realistic with you—for the most part, mental illness does not just go away. Yes, God performed miracles in our life, but there is always going to be an aspect of mental illness that we will deal with. I do not want to set the precedent that God will take it all away because that is His choice, not mine; mental illness is not a flu. You do not just recover and it goes away. We are so thankful that God has given us the ability to control it better and we are still learning where the limits are when it pops its head out at us.

Our goal is to give a resource of tangible ways that people can get out of the darkness and seek help if necessary. If you're the spouse or loved one of someone struggling, we hope this resource will help you on that very difficult road, too. We have committed to following what we believe God is asking us to do by sharing our story and opening the door to letting us help others and lead them back to God with it.

In this book I will walk you through ways to endure the dark times in the role as the supporter of someone with mental illness. I also want to examine who the enemy really is, because he is the root of darkness and sin in this world, and as much as there are people who struggle, he is where it all begins and who uses opportunities to keep it alive. After we take a critical look at who the enemy is, we will look at what we can do in the situation, ways we can help the person we love in the situation, and things to know about being in the situation of supporting someone struggling with mental illness. In the end, I hope you come out with a passionate relationship with God, a stronger marriage or relationship, and hopefully some ways to manage the other side of this disease of mental illness.

Chapter 1: Exposing the Enemy

Put on the full armor of God, so that you can take your stand against the devil's schemes. For our struggle is not against flesh and blood, but against the rulers, against the authorities, against the powers of this dark world and against the spiritual forces of evil in the heavenly realms. Therefore put on the full armor of God, so that when the day of evil comes, you may be able to stand your ground, and after you have done everything, to stand. Stand firm then, with the belt of truth buckled around your waist, with the breastplate of righteousness in place, and with your feet fitted with the readiness that comes from the gospel of peace. In addition to all this, take up the shield of faith, with which you can extinguish all the flaming arrows of the evil one. Take the helmet of salvation and the sword of the Spirit, which is the word of God (Ephesians 6:11-17).

The first topic we are going to dive into is the enemy. Satan preys on people who struggle because they are much more vulnerable to his schemes. I really don't have anything nice to say at all about Satan—nobody does. He is evil, deceitful, prideful, and a liar. He is sadly smart and has been at this job for centuries and has found ways to get what he wants. I want to share with you a secret I learned that has helped me tremendously: The closer we are to God, the easier it is to see Satan's work. As we fall away from God, Satan's work starts to look a lot more real or normal. Now please don't give Satan any more credit or power than he deserves. He may look smart, but remember that he is a deceiver, too! That's right, he *looks* smart, but what is he really? Let's look to the Bible and get the answers there.

The Other Side of the Struggle

> You belong to your father, the devil, and you want to carry out your father's desires. He was a murderer from the beginning, not holding to the truth, for there is no truth in him. When he lies, he speaks his native language, for he is a liar and the father of lies (John 8:44).

> The thief comes only to steal and kill and destroy; I came that they may have life, and have it to the full (John 10:10).

> The one who does what is sinful is of the devil, because the devil has been sinning from the beginning. The reason the Son of God appeared was to destroy the devil's work (1 John 3:8).

Here is the truth: Satan is the father of lies; he is a fraud; he is a thief who is here to steal, kill, and destroy. It is hard to believe that people willingly fall into this, but we all do because we all have sin nature inside of us. As I said earlier, the further you are away from your relationship with God, the easier it is to be deceived because you do not have the protection around your mind to ward off the enemy's attacks. But he is the father of lies—that means that he is good at what he does and he gets personal. He knows what to say and where to attack each person specifically to find a weakness to break them. A friend of mine said something to me that puts Satan in perspective: Satan is on a leash. It may seem like he is powerful, that he can overtake our lives with his evilness, but he is on a leash and God is the one holding that leash. He can only go so far until his limits are reached. Remember that when you are feeling consumed by his efforts—God is already victorious over him and he can only get so far. That helped me take away a lot of the power I was giving him in my own head.

The main area Satan attacks me is through my husband. He has footholds on my husband like I have never seen before. He has so ingrained lies into my husband's head that some days even I almost believe them. Satan will use his grip on my husband to also take me down and get us both with one shot. It is the craziest cycle I have ever experienced, but it's worked for centuries and that's why he keeps doing it. Because we are letting it work. The fact that Satan has been at this for so long can either scare us or inform us. Yes, he may be skilled at it, but his ways are predictable; he has no new material, just a different avenue to use the same old deception. When you are able to change the way you think about Satan it takes away the power that fear of him had over you.

As you walk through a difficult battle with someone close to you struggling with mental illness, the enemy will do everything in his power to keep you from relying on God. This is why it is important to spend a little bit of time focusing on getting to know the enemy so we can become aware of who he is and his ways and be better able to protect our hearts, minds, and souls from his attacks. We are going to look at some of the enemy's strategic battle plans and expose them before we even get started. If you know where the attacks generate from, they are much easier to fight against.

When you are in a war, it is important to know as much about the enemy as you can in order to understand him, know his weaknesses and boundaries, and how he is going to attack you so you can prepare yourself. The battle I am talking about is not a physical battle but a spiritual and mental battle— an unseen battle. This is much harder to fight against because is invisible in a tangible way, but it is there and it is real and we need to take it as seriously as if it were a physical war on our soil.

Before we dig deep into what it is like to be on the other side of the struggle of mental illness, I want to take a moment and break down who the actual enemy is and look at his goals to destroy you, the weapons he will use against you, the strategies he will use to try and break you down, and who he is and what characteristics create him to be the enemy that he is. It is important to understand that when you are focusing on the enemy you need to pray for protection over your mind so you only focus an appropriate amount of energy and time on Satan, allowing your true focus to be geared toward God. It is okay to research and educate yourself about the beast we are dealing with, but focusing too much time on him is not only a distraction but is also unhealthy for your spiritual walk.

Goals

First, I want to look at Satan's goals. What are his aspirations? What are his objectives, hopes, and desires when he attacks us? I have come up with a list of the enemy's goals that I call "The 7 Ds." You see, knowing what his motives are and what he is trying to do helps us form a defense strategy. The first step we need to take is a step back. If that seems backward, it's because it is! We need to stop and examine where the enemy is coming from in order to gain perspective about the type of battle we are in.

The 7 Ds

1. Destroy Faith

This is one of Satan's primary goals. He wants this more than we want great riches. He salivates like a dog wanting a treat; he hungers for it and all his motives come back to this key goal. His main goal is to demolish people's faith and abolish it from existence. Satan is only allowed to prowl around earth and hell, so if he accomplished this goal, he could have free rein to control and authority over every person and every thing.

2. Deny the Battle

It's pretty easy for Satan to win the battle if he can make you believe there isn't one to begin with! It is like being in school and a friend was being bullied but didn't even know it; wouldn't that enrage you? (It should.) Another example is to accept that mental illness is what it is and that there is nothing you can do about it—that you have to accept the way things are even if they are negative. That is exactly the place that Satan wants you to be—accepting that it "is what it is" and that you can't do anything about it. That is what Satan will try to get you to believe if you are not certain that the battle is real. If you allow Satan into your mind about this one, just read Ephesians 6:11-12. The Bible is very clear about the reality of the spiritual battles that we face. But if you tend to learn lessons the hard way (like me), then have at it, but trust me when I tell you from many experiences on the front lines—the battle is real.

3. Divide God's People

Be aware that all relationships are at stake for the enemy's attack. The more division Satan can create, the less of a team (we'll call it "God's team") he has to fight. The more people he can pick off from that number, the less work he has to do. I have seen Satan attack my relationship with my husband, my mother, and even my children to try and pit us against each other! The less bonded we are, the less united we become—and that is where Satan tries to weasel his way in and cause bitterness, anger, slander, and unforgiveness. He has an even bigger goal then this—most of all he wants division in the church. The Bible says he is like a lion ready to devour his prey; the church is his prey and he is lurking in the shadows of each and every conversation and relationship, hoping to jump out and strike. He is an opportunist and will attack when least expected. If you are ever feeling like leaving your church, please filter your reasons through people you trust to look at the situation objectively and clearly to see if Satan is just meddling or if there is a reasonable cause for doing so.

4. Deceive Every Mind

"And no wonder, for Satan himself masquerades as an angel of light" (2 Corinthians 11:14). You see, Satan is the father of lies and a deceiver. He will do anything he can to deceive your mind into believing anything but God's Word. Have you ever justified a sin you committed? Have you ever thought, *Oh, it's not that bad*, or, *It's not as bad as what so-and-so did*. When we allow our minds to be open to the things of this world, if we are not focusing on God's Word like it is our lifeline, Satan will be attacking our minds like nothing we have ever experienced before. His deception is extensive and has no limits—from more obvious ways like occult practices to much sneakier and "sly" avenues. One thing I have heard many times is that we are most vulnerable when we are ignorant about this deception. First Peter 5:8-9 warns us to, "Be alert and of sober mind. Your enemy the devil prowls around like a roaring lion looking for someone to devour. Resist him, standing firm in the faith, because you know that the family of believers throughout the world is undergoing the same kind of sufferings."

5. Direct into False Teaching

Here is the tough part about false teaching—it doesn't sound like false teaching. It sounds good! It sounds real. It sounds right—but it's not. I don't know enough about this topic to go into great detail, and I do not like to write about what I am not greatly knowledgeable about but I will elaborate a bit. First John 4:1 talks about discerning false prophets. "Dear friends, do not believe every spirit, but test the spirits to see whether they are from God, because many false prophets have gone out into the world." Matthew 7:15-20 goes on to talk about how false prophets will come disguised as sheep but are really wolves and how we can detect them by the way they act, by the fruit of their spirit. I have done a little bit of research and found some very interesting things about being a "fruit inspector" as John Upchurch calls it. Like the Bible says, we have to "test them." Where is their information coming from? If it is not the Bible that is their primary source—that is a red flag. If they are focusing on outside sources more than biblically sound truth, that is another red flag. Are they changing sound doctrinal truths like God's character or other black-and-white doctrine of the Bible? This gives us another red flag. False teachers use the right words, flashy presentations, and appealing arguments, but there will always be something that doesn't seem quite right. Do not be afraid to question everything.

6. Distract from God

How busy is your schedule? Between working, kids, schedules, appointments, eating, and getting ready to do it all over again the next day, our time goes by in the blink of an eye. That is Satan's goal. That is why it is so important to sacrifice the best time of our day and spend it with God. For me it is early in the morning—instead of that last little bit of sleep I can get, I pull myself out of bed and go into my prayer room. If you find yourself rushing your prayer time, doing it just to check it off your list, skipping it altogether, or being so busy you even forget about it, that is a red flag that Satan is at work! Take things off your plate and put time aside because you will never win the battle if you are not investing time with the One who provides the strength, endurance, and protection you need for the fight.

7. Dilute Our Efforts

Have you ever heard a small voice in your head saying things like, "You can't do it," "You're not able to do that on your own; you're just one person," "Nothing you are doing is making a difference," or "You don't have the power to change anything"? These are lies that Satan is using to make you feel insignificant and powerless compared to what you are actually able to do in God's strength—and he knows it! His best strategy is to make you feel like you can't do what you need to do, because if he can make you freeze in fear and failure then he will feel victorious in accomplishing his goals. Don't give him that satisfaction. God has given me a dream many times in my life, and Satan has diluted my efforts in my own mind so many times that I took the wrong path away from what God wanted me to do. Writing this book was a step for me to finally ignore that lie and take a leap of faith, risking much to be obedient to what God was calling me to do.

Take Away

Things to Take Away from This Chapter:

Satan's goals: The 7 Ds

1. Destroy Faith
2. Deny the Battle
3. Divide God's People
4. Deceive Every Mind
5. Direct into False Teaching
6. Distract from God
7. Dilute our Efforts

Chapter 2: Characteristics of the Enemy

N ow I want to look at who Satan is and how we can get to know him so well that his attacks become predictable and expected. Knowing the characteristics and traits that he is composed of allows us to fully know who we are dealing with. The definition of a *characteristic* is, "A distinguishing feature or quality."[2]

Liar

> You belong to your father, the devil, and you want to carry out your father's desires. He was a murderer from the beginning, not holding to the truth, for there is no truth in him. When he lies, he speaks his native language, for he is a liar and the father of lies (John 8:44).

Satan is a fabricator of the truth who will say anything to get you away from God and away from the light.

Prideful

> Your heart became proud on account of your beauty, and you corrupted your wisdom because of your splendor. So I threw you to the earth; I made a spectacle of you before kings (Ezekiel 28:17).

> Pride goes before destruction, a haughty spirit before a fall (Proverbs 16:18).

2. Dictionary.com Unabridged, s.v. "characteristic," Random House, Inc., http://www.dictionary. com/browse/characteristic (accessed: June 7, 2017).

The Other Side of the Struggle

Pride is the initial characteristic that caused Satan to be separated from God. This was where it all began. It comes before the fall. I would even go as far to say that pride is one of his biggest distinguishing traits.

Evil

> The thief comes only to steal and kill and destroy (John 10:10).

Satan is cruel, he is wicked, and he is immoral. I don't know about you, but what John is saying about him seems pretty evil to me.

Deceiver

> The great dragon was hurled down—that ancient serpent called the devil, or Satan, who leads the whole world astray. He was hurled to the earth, and his angels with him (Revelation 12:9).

Satan deceives us because that is who he is—he was cast out of heaven and his office is earth. He deceives us for his own personal advantage. He will double-cross you without thinking; He will cheat or trick you into thinking or behaving in ways that benefit him because of this characteristic.

Imitator

> And no wonder, for Satan himself masquerades as an angel of light (2 Corinthians 11:14).

Satan is a fake; he can manipulate your mind to make you believe things that are not true, he can convince you it's real, and the unfortunate part is that he is pretty good at it. He can mimic, emulate, and simulate things so that you see it the way he wants you to see it.

Accuser

> Now have come the salvation and the power and the kingdom of our God, and the authority of his Messiah. For the accuser of our brothers and sisters, who accuses them before our God day and night, has been hurled down (Revelation 12:10).

We see a great example of this in Job. Satan is more or less a tattletale to God; he accuses us as if we are in court, pointing out what we do wrong. Then he gloats when he gets to do this. It's part of his defense, but don't worry—God is not fooled by this; He knows this is who Satan is.

Schemer

> In order that Satan might not outwit us. For we are not unaware of his schemes (2 Corinthians 2:11).

Satan is a sneaky fiend; he is devious, a plotter, and a politician. He manipulates his schemes to seem what they are not, and he always has an agenda.

Enticer

> "You will not certainly die," the serpent said to the woman. "For God knows that when you eat from it your eyes will be opened, and you will be like God, knowing good and evil." When the woman saw that the fruit of the tree was good for food and pleasing to the eye, and also desirable for gaining wisdom, she took some and ate it. She also gave some to her husband, who was with her, and he ate it (Genesis 3:4-6).

Satan is a persuader; he is charismatic and charming. You don't think you are being enticed until it's all over and you look back, shocked how you even believed for a second. He is convincing and he makes it attractive. If you look at history, you will find terrible leaders who had millions of followers. Those people weren't stupid—they were persuaded by an illusion.

Tempter

> And he was in the wilderness forty days, being tempted by Satan. He was with the wild animals, and angels attended him (Mark 1:13).

Satan even goes so far as to tempt Jesus! One of his core characteristics is a tempter. He allures us with personal things we are vulnerable to and sins that take us away from God. He will use anything to tempt you. He has even manages to make good things bad when he baits us with our desires and then twists them so we put them before God.

Oppressor

> Be alert and of sober mind. Your enemy the devil prowls around like a roaring lion looking for someone to devour (1 Peter 5:8).

When we are vulnerable, Satan will attack us like Peter tells us in the verse above. He likes to keep us down by his oppressive authority, trying to overwhelm and crush us so we follow him and not God.

Take Away

Things to Take Away from This Chapter:

Satan's Characteristics:

Liar
Prideful
Evil
Deceiver
Imitator
Accuser
Schemer
Enticer
Tempter
Oppressor

Chapter 3: Weapons and Strategies of the Enemy

Weapons

N ext we are going to look at the weapons Satan brings to battle. As a solider going into battle, he gathers his weapons to defend himself. Because Satan's weapons are not as easy to see as a sword or gun, it is important to educate ourselves on what they are so we do not get taken out by the enemy's weapon without seeing it coming.

The definition of a weapon is "an instrument for use in an attack; anything used against an opponant."[3]

Unforgiveness, Anger, and Bitterness

This weapon is characterized by strong feelings of displeasure, resentfulness, hostility, and cynicism. These are things that if they are not dealt with will lead to hate, grudges, and resentment—the perfect recipe Satan uses to keep your mind so angry that you wouldn't dare turn to God. A heart that has unforgiveness and bitterness in it becomes cold and dark and is Satan's perfect playground.

Disappointment

The weapon of disappointment brings failure, defeat, and frustration. You will feel like you are disappointing your family, friends, or peers when this weapon is used. Another way Satan loves to use this one is to make you feel like you are a disappointment to God—that you can't measure up and there

---

3. Dictionary.com Unabridged, s.v. "weapon," Random House, Inc., http://www.dictionary.com/browse/weapon (accessed: June 7, 2017).

is no point in trying. Satan may also use this weapon by getting you to feel disappointed with things in life, with your job, your circumstances, your body, and so on. (That list can go on and on, right?) We become frustrated when things don't change the way we want; we become defeated when we try to do something but don't succeed. This instrument makes us feel like a failure and convinces us that we cannot turn to God as a failure.

Discouragement

The effects of this weapon are a deterrent, an obstruction, and feelings of dejection. This weapon has been at work when you feel like you are trying your hardest, doing everything right, and you still are not getting the results you are looking for. It is when obstacles keep turning up and the waves keep hitting you. This weapon is designed to make you vulnerable. The more hoops you have to jump, the more deterrents on your path, the more tired you become, the more discouraged you get, leaving you vulnerable. Weak and defenseless is exactly where the enemy wants you because his strategies work so much better when you are in such a frail state.

Depression

This weapon causes emotional dejection, withdrawal, and isolation. Satan uses this armament by making you feel like there is no hope and no promise in the future. It's very hard to move forward when you are feeling hopeless. He sometimes is able to use this weapon to completly overtake a person's life to the point where they can't function. This is his ideal scenario because when you are succumbed to darkness, it is very hard to see the light. Another instrument he uses within this is isolation. Satan loves to get you to isolate yourself from others because then he can be the only voice in your head. Don't be surprised when you are feeling down and out that you don't want to be around anyone and just want to segregate yourself from everyone in your life. If you are feeling that way, remind yourself that Satan is likely behind that feeling.

Debt

This weapon makes you a slave because you owe something to someone; you become legally responsible for something. Debt becomes a stronghold over us. It keeps us in chains to the lender, which is exactly where Satan likes us to be. It's harder to fight back when we are being held back by chains. Usually when we talk about debt it is in financial terms, but debt can happen in a variety of ways.

Impatience and Busyness

This common weapon creates feelings of intolerance, irritability, restlessness, engaged activity, and everything seems cluttered. I don't know about you, but my impatience brings out the worst in me. I snap at my kids and my husband without even thinking; I am short with my words and hurtful with my behavior. I'm far from being honest with God about life when I am in an impatient mood, which is exactly how this weapon strikes. When we become restless with our life, we are taking ourselves out of the stillness we must have in Christ. Satan plays on your emotions when using this weapon and it's really scary how easily it works some days. This is where busyness works perfectly with his schemes. It is hard to fit in time to sit still in the presence of God when your plate is overloaded and you're stressed about how to get it all done. The thing about busyness is that Satan doesn't have to do a lot to involve this weapon; all he has to do is facilitate this environment and we pretty much do the rest ourselves.

Worry and Fear

This onslaught gets us to feel uneasy, concerned, anxious, distressed, troubled, feeling like we are in danger, causing apprehension, terror, and panic. When we worry, we are taking our trust away from God and focusing on the negative. This weapon works by distracting our mind. Even though there are things we cannot control, things that may make us anxious, worrisome, or even fearful, we must recognize they are not from God—they are straight from the enemy, distracting you from God and the good He is doing. Fear can make a person do things they never thought they would do. Fear is controlling; it pushes you up against a wall and forces you to give in when you likely would not under normal circumstances. Fear is one of Satan's top weapons that has a very high success rate.

Doubt

This weapon causes us to feel skeptical. It comes with disbelief, distrust, uncertainty, and confusion. Sometimes I can literally feel doubt seeping into my brain; it's like a part of my brain let down its guard for a moment and doubt snuck in. Doubt can come in all forms. Doubting God, His realness, questioning His power, doubting His love. A subcategory of doubt is the belief in false religions. Satan doesn't care what religion you are believing as long as it's not Christianity, so he will make you question it and "connect" more with another belief system, maybe one that fits more comfortably in your sinful lifestyle. When researching the word *doubt,* the word *confusion* comes up. There are times in my life when I get confused about the gospel, especially when I am explaining it to people, and it makes me feel uneducated and unknowledgeable. In turn, I am also relaying confusion to whoever I am speaking to, causing disbelief in them as well. This ends up killing two birds with one stone for the enemy.

Pride

This weapon creates an unhealthy amount of ownership, dignity, value, and confidence. We all, Christian or not, have struggled with, are struggling with, and will struggle again with pride. Pride comes in many shapes and sizes and it is Satan's favorite weapon because, as we saw earlier, it is the foundation of who Satan is. It comes in forms of confidence, conceit, and egocentric behavior and thinking. It is characterized by believing you are better than others, that you are above them. It comes in forms of expectation and entitlement, latching on to your character and personality. If you don't fight it off, it will try to live there forever.

Envy and Jealousy

These weapons involve grudging adoration, resenting others, longing, inadequacy, and the fear of losing. These two are other artilleries used in the battle. Longing for what others have and the "keeping up with the Joneses" mentality are where we see them in today's culture. We all want more, yet will never be satisfied even if we gain bigger houses, more money, or more things. Satan has successfully overtaken our culture and society in envy. Media alone subliminally drills this into our heads. Jealousy, on the other hand, is focused more on resentment and fear of losing. It does entail jealousy of others as envy does, but it also finds a nice home in relationships—especially marriages. Satan hates marriage, especially Christian ones, so jealously is a sly little tool he uses to cause destruction of trust and spite in relationships.

Strategies

Satan's strategies are the last area we are going to focus on the enemy. Then we are going to move on from him; we have spent a lot of time and energy on him and that's enough. A strategy is a plan of action or policy designed to achieve a major or overall aim. Satan attacks in five main methods using different and personal tactics.

1. Strategies of Temptation

Satan and his soldiers will study you specifically and personally until they can pinpoint your weaknesses; then they customize a plan that encompasses your wants, desires, and vulnerabilities in an attempt to take you down.

In the day and age we live in, there are literally endless ways he can use this tactic. There are three main ways he will try to get you with temptation—body, mind, and spirit.

- **Body.** This is one we can all understand; we have all seen this one pretty clearly in our society. It is evident in lust, cheating, pornography, media propaganda, and so on. Our world is filled with this type of temptation. It's the easiest one to see. The Bible says, "Offer your bodies as a living sacrifice, holy and pleasing to God— this is your true and proper worship" (Romans 12:1).

- **Mind.** This is a tough one to catch at first glance. I get caught in this one all the time. Things like social media, TV, and overuse of our smartphones are ways that the enemy gets our mind distracted from God. The Bible says, " Do not conform to the pattern of this world, but be transformed by the renewing of your mind" (Romans 12:2).

- **Spirit.** Satan uses tactics such as pride, power, and busyness to attack your spirit. If you are getting too busy to spend time with God, you are under attack. If you are too successful to feel like you need your God, you are under attack. If you are feeling like you can do it all on your own, you are under attack. The Bible says, " Do not think of yourself more highly than you ought, but rather think of yourself with sober judgment, in accordance with the faith God has distributed to each of you" (Romans 12:3).

2. Strategies of Lies and Half-Truths

> Be alert and of sober mind. Your enemy the devil prowls around
> like a roaring lion looking for someone to devour (1 Peter 5:8).

Here's what I know about lies from my own experiences. Satan ingrains a lie into your mind. That's all the work he has to really do because we do the rest for him and he doesn't have to lift a finger! For example, let's say the lie is "I am not worthy of love." Each time any experience you encounter remotely resembles that lie, like if you get your heart broken in a relationship, that lie gets reiterated as being a truth. Over time and years of going on like this, the lie is no longer a lie in your mind but a truth, and it is very hard to break that cycle. Thankfully, we serve a God who can break apart any lie, no matter how deep and ingrained it is in your head.

Satan starts to put these lies in your head from the childhood. As you grow up and start to learn about the world, he is there waiting and scheming, using every opportunity he possibly can. He even goes so far as to use the problems from your parents. Now that I am a parent I see this even more clearly. I see my own lies and my husband's lies being passed down to our daughters as truths! They don't even have the opportunity to realize it's a lie because we didn't deal with it properly ourselves, so now we are passing lies down generationally.

The only reason that Satan speaks the truth is to deceive. This is where "half-truths" come into play. He will leave a little bit of the truth intertwined in the lie to make it more convincing and believable. For a couple months before we were married, my husband and I tried living together. We tried to justify our actions the entire time and it was a nightmare. It doesn't directly say in the Bible, "Do not live with your boyfriend or girlfriend before marriage," but God knows that we have sin nature in us and that we do not always stand strong in the wake of temptation and that by presenting the temptation of living together before marriage we are much more likely to give into the temptation.

Because Satan tied a little truth and lie together, we believe it would be okay for our marriage to indulge in aspects of a relationship that are only intended for marriage. In the end, we were deeply convicted and the situation turned out to be so bad that when we moved to a new town we ended up living apart until we were married. After being married I look back at how special it is and I understand why God designed it this way. At the time, I fell into Satan's trap of believing the half-truths he was whispering into my ear.

3. Strategies of Deception and Intimidation

Opposition

Have you even felt opposition from people close to you? When I am walking in obedience to God's will for my life, I get opposition from the craziest sources—people close to me! It is such a good strategy because it throws you off guard and makes you question what God wants you to do. It hits so close to home that if you are not standing on solid ground in Christ, it works.

Patronization and Belittling

Satan wants you to feel unimportant, that you don't matter, and that you cannot make a difference. With this strategy he can stop you in your tracks from following God's call on your life because you don't feel adequate enough to do it. He takes away your confidence in God by doing this so that you don't live up to the potential God has for you.

Ignorance

I can't tell you how many times I didn't follow something I felt God calling me to do because I felt a lack of knowledge and understanding to do it or even talk about it. This was the case even with writing. I thought, *Who am I to claim the things I am saying?* These are the thoughts Satan strategically puts in our minds so that we don't follow God, and we stay in a stagnant place of doing nothing.

Imitation

We have concluded that Satan is an imitator, but he uses this strategy in the action of disguising things to look similar to what God wants you to do so that it tricks you. This strategy got us when we were trying to decide what to do with our careers. I have always known that God has a plan for my life, and He gives me little pieces of it each time I walk in obedience with Him. As we were in a pivotal time in our life trying to decided what to do, Satan used key aspects of what we were looking for in a career and imitated a plan that looked very similar to what God had showed me. It was convincing and looked like a great plan from the outside, so we took a big risk and followed it. The problem was, there was no room for God in this plan, and it became quite clear to me that this was not from God and we had been tricked. It was a very hard lesson to learn because we truly thought we were doing the right thing.

4. Strategies of Fear

Fear makes us do things we likely would not do in normal circumstances. It makes us question what our morals really are if we would make decisions differently out of fear. A big one most of us are scared of is the end times and what will happen at the end of the world. It is scary, but doesn't that determine who we should be and how we live? The answer should be no, but according to Satan it is yes. Some fears are ingrained in us from childhood, some are common fears like being scared of flying in planes, and some fears have attached themselves into our character and become part of us, like fear of upsetting people or fear of confrontation. Others go even deeper into fear of failure, fear of commitment, or fear of love. The Bible tells us over and over "Do not be afraid" and that fear is not from God. So when you are afraid, you need to hold that feeling accountable and those thoughts captive and run them through a filter, asking yourself, "Who is this from?" "Who does it benefit if I give in to these feelings?" and "Is this from God?" Most of the time answering those questions can allow you to recognize an attack and give you the confidence and freedom to disengage from it entirely.

5. Strategies of Theft and Murder

Satan steals our mind by enticing us with our earthy sinful desires. He steals our mind away from God and murders our soul in the process. He steals our joy, our passions, and our happiness.

***

This is the end of the journey of exposing the enemy. I have said this before but will say it again: Don't focus too much on Satan; don't give him too much power. He is already defeated by God. We went through this journey to educate ourselves about who we are dealing with in the battle.

Things to Take Away from This Chapter:

Satan's Weapons

Unforgiveness, Anger, Bitterness
Disappointment
Discouragement
Depression
Debt
Worry and Fear
Doubt
Pride
Envy and Jealousy

Satan's Strategies

Strategies of Temptation
Strategies of Lies and Half-Truths
Strategies of Deception and Intimidation
Strategies of Fear
Strategies of Theft and Murder

Chapter 4: Pray

This is really the best piece of advice I can offer you. Everything else comes from what I have learned along the way, but this is the most crucial information I can give you. I was once asked if God was my steering wheel or my spare tire. I encourage you to ask yourself this and be as honest as you can. Do you run to Him only when you are in need, or are you pouring into that relationship daily to fill you up every day? When do you find it easiest and hardest to rely on God? Do you ever struggle to spend time with Him or rely on Him in difficult times?

I find when things are difficult, when I am experiencing hardship, I grab on to God's rope without even thinking. It becomes my lifeline and my life support. In the midst of a struggle or on the front line of the battlefield, I have no doubt in my mind that God is who I need to turn to. Then when things start going great again, all the glory goes to God. I am praising and glorifying Him over and over again. But I find that it is during the between time, when life is just happening, where Satan likes to attack and make me think that I don't need God anymore.

What is really crazy is how powerful and convincing Satan is when he attacks our feelings. I find myself not as eager to get out of bed to read my Bible in the morning, and I keep pushing snooze, no longer sacrificing that time to get up and read my Bible and talk to my heavenly Father before my day begins and my kids wake up. I find I am not as joyful to engage in different areas where I know God wants me to be. This makes sense because as I am not spending time with Him, I am not close to Him. I don't feel the hunger to seek His direction and guidance in where I should be walking. Distractions are the easiest way for Satan to make this happen. Social media and all the technology in this generation make it so easy to get sucked into this state of being. I can start to feel myself not being able to put my phone down when I get on to social media. I am not saying social media is a bad thing; anything can be a distraction—good or bad—when it becomes more important or replaces time that should be spent pouring into and building up your relationship with God. Don't let the enemy take your relationship with God; nothing he can offer you will ever satisfy you because it is all false and fake. The saying "it is too good to be true" is exactly the case here. The only thing real you can rely on is God.

Picture someone you are very close to, like a parent or a very good friend. Now imagine that you never talked to them on a regular basis, only calling when you needed things like money. I used to do this to my parents, and I can personally tell you that it is not a relationship but a one-way expectation that is based on your own needs and wants. It is selfish, self-centered, and makes the relationship turn cold. It's the same if we never spend regular time with God and just come to Him when things aren't going so well. It's hurtful and disrespectful to the relationship and also isn't going to get you anywhere in the long run. To combat this, I had to set up guidelines of what I wanted my relationship to be like. I wanted to spend time with Him daily, so that is a goal I made for myself. I also wanted creative ways to spend time with Him so I don't get caught in the trap of spending time with Him just because it is part of my routine.

What are some ways you spend pouring into your relationship with God? We are human; it's okay to accept we are not perfect and won't have any perfect answers. All He asks is we come to Him trying.

When you have someone in your life who struggles with something as unpredictable as mental illness, you have to understand that you are dealing with something bigger than yourself. When you are in the midst of a battle, this is when prayer needs to become your lifeline. I don't mean pray as in "please change them, God," but I mean fervent, continuous, all-consuming prayer. I mean prayer that causes you to listen and obey what God asks you to do. I am talking about prayer that is as important as food and water in your daily life. I got to the point where I made a "war room" in my basement and literally lived there every moment when I wasn't working or parenting. I encourage you to find a spot where you can spend time with God; I don't care where you do it, but do it. God is the only One who can fix the problems in your life. So take it to Him, give it to Him, and leave it at the cross. It's the hardest thing you will do because it's our nature to problem-solve and try to fix things ourselves. But doing that won't get you anywhere.

We need to look at our heart when we come to God asking for help. I asked Him to change our situation for years in the wrong heart, and nothing happened. When I learned this concept of how important it is to "come" with the right heart to the Lord, things changed instantly. You need to be willing to change, willing and open for however God is going to respond to the situation. Sometimes we ask for help but are expecting Him to answer the prayer in the exact way we feel is right. Then when He does answer us in a different way, we either don't recognize it or disregard that He even came into the situation at all.

The other part of praying is knowing that God will show you things you need to change in order for the situation to get better. It's hard to hear, but be open to it; He knows what He's talking about. Each time I have asked God to change someone else, the first thing He always comes back with is something *I* need to change. It is hard because our focus is so intensely looking at the other person, at their problems and how big they seem, that we get humbled because we need to change our focus and look within. We tend to compare the smaller issues we are having with those big things the other person is dealing with. God cares just as much about your well-being, and even though the intensity or scale of the problems seems so far apart, God does not see it that way. We are the ones who create levels of sin and categorize one type of sin as bigger than another. But in God's eyes any sin is wrong, no matter how small or severe we think it is. God knows that there are things you need to change that will help change the situation. You are the only one you can control, so it is very important to listen to Him when He is asking something of you. He always knows best, even though sometimes we don't understand it.

If you were going into a real battle in a war, you would not go alone. We are not intended to walk the trials of life by ourselves. You need to create an army—a prayer army. Find others to pray with you. There is power in numbers; there is power in crying out to God together. I encourage you to find people you are comfortable with sharing what you are going through and enlist them as prayer warriors. Not only can they pray for the situation, for the other person who is struggling, but they can also support you in prayer. You need prayer to get through just as much as the person who is struggling does. You need the strength and courage to keep going on and to not fall apart yourself, so having people praying for you is incredibly important as you walk the journey.

Find other ways to come to the Lord. It doesn't always need to be sitting and praying. There were some songs that came to me in some really dark times that worked in such powerful ways and brought me closer to Him. There are so many ways we can worship our God, and these are forms of prayer and worship, so don't close yourself in a box and feel like the "traditional" way to pray is the only option. God created us all to be different; we all connect to Him in different ways.

I encourage you to be specific in your prayers. Even though God always knows what you are asking and what you are talking about without you having to say it, it is important to name our requests. Being specific is a good way to organize your thoughts in the situation. It also helps to focus in on certain issues that you need to hone in on with God as you work things out. As we come to Him with specific prayers, write them out and speak them out loud. There is power in this action. It is also really amazing to re-read them occasionally because after some time has passed you can see how things have progressed since you wrote it out. You can see where your heart was in the moment you read it and hopefully see how far the situation has come since then.

Take Away

Things to Take Away from This Chapter:

- Fervent prayer will fill you up and give you the energy and strength to keep going.
- You need to pray as though prayer is just as important as food and water.
- Be specific—write and speak it out.
- You need prayer warriors to lean on and to pray with you.
- Is God your steering wheel or spare tire?
- Be aware of the distractions that Satan will set up.
- Respect your relationship with God. Sacrifice the best time of your day back to Him.
- Create your own prayer space that is sacred for your time with God.
- Get creative and worship Him in different ways.

Chapter 5: God Is Real, No Matter How I Feel

There are two times in life when we feel like God isn't there. The first is when we have turned away from Him. The second is when God pulls back to see how we react and cope without Him. It's best described as God's test to see how serious we are when we say that we trust Him completely. Are we still able to follow Him when we don't feel His presence? Here is the problem: We as humans succumb to our "feelings." God does not leave us, but there are certainly times we feel like He has. This is part of the enemy's tactic; he preys on our feelings because that is where we are vulnerable and able to be swayed.

God says, "I will never leave you or forsake you," so when you feel an absence from God, I encourage you to seriously ask yourself, "Who has left whom?" It's very black and white. He promises to never leave us, so when we are trying to find out why we are feeling the distance, we need to turn the perspective around and look within. We need to look at ourselves. What are we doing? How are we behaving? How are we spending our time? How much effort are we putting into our relationship with God?

The Bible says, "I will wait for the Lord, who is hiding his face from the descendants of Jacob. I will put my trust in him" (Isaiah 8:17). In the midst of sorrow is probably the hardest time to feel like God is there. In his book *The Purpose Driven Life*, Rick Warren says, "The deepest level of worship is praising God in spite of pain, thanking God during a trial, trusting him when tempted, surrendering while suffering, and loving him when he seems distant." [4] Many emotions come up when we feel like God is not with us, especially in times of suffering: anger, hurt, abandonment, fear, loneliness, and worry. But we are not the only people who struggle with this. Even David felt this way. He wrote such things as, "Lord why are You standing aloof and far away? Why do You hide when I need You the most? Why have You forsaken me? Why do You remain so distant? Why do You ignore my cries for help? Why have You abandoned me?"

Job is another example of someone in the Bible who went through times of not feeling God's presence. There were moments when Job felt alone and abandoned by everyone, even God, but he still never spoke against God even though his circumstances and the people around him were encouraging him to. As Job cries out, God is silent, but that does not mean He isn't there. It is important to recognize these examples in the Bible because we serve the same God Job and David served, and because we can see the victory they experienced we can trust that God has the same love and plans for our lives.

Here is where it becomes so difficult—when we are going through a trial, through suffering, through something so difficult that it seems like our world is falling apart, when it may be difficult to even get through an hour, let alone a day. Those are moments when distance from God can become part of making the situation worse very quickly if we are not careful. The enemy can get a foothold in these situations so quickly. We have to remember that he is an opportunist and will attack at our most vulnerable moments, and he does not wait for our permission. The first thing to remember when something difficult happens in our life is that it is normal as humans to have the feelings we are experiencing, that it is okay to allow ourselves to walk through these feelings but to keep in mind we have two choices. The first choice we have is to allow the enemy to gain a foothold in the situation—to allow the situation to destroy you and overtake your life and to walk away from the God who loves you even despite the circumstances occurring. The second choice you have is to allow yourself to walk through the difficult storm and

4. Rick Warren, *The Purpose-Driven Life,* (Grand Rapids, MI: Zondervan: 2002), 100-112.

understand the battle you are in. This choice is to fight back, not letting yourself be a soldier who has thrown in the towel but one who has put their armor on to protect themselves from the enemy. Part of this is also to learn and grow where God is teaching.

From my own trials, I have learned that there is always a lesson and a purpose in whatever you are experiencing. God does not waste one tear you shed, and He is always putting things in place to hold you through the storm, even when you don't feel it. The other part of going through trials is to know that many times we don't see the big picture while we are in the midst of it. In the middle of the storm, the waves are high and strong. It is not always that easy to see the purpose, the lessons, or the bigger picture while in the middle of it. There is a beautiful song that came to me in one of my darkest moments and helped me through the difficult battle I was enduring. It spoke to me saying, "If you are going to focus on the storm, you will question My love and My truth. If you focus on Me, your God and Savior, you'll know that I have always been there, will always be there, and will never let you down." It really spoke to me because it showed me that we have a choice, and it is not an easy choice. We can decide to focus on the negative, the storm and the situation, or we can focus on God, His promise, His track record, and His purpose. I can tell you that once we change our way of thinking about the situation, we start to see God working a lot faster than if we allow ourselves to be engulfed by the terribleness of the situation. Something that really helped me once I started to change my thinking was looking at what the Bible says about suffering, and it actually encouraged and strengthened me and even made me feel important that I would be going through something difficult because God had a bigger plan.

> Not only so, but we also glory in our sufferings, because we know that suffering produces perseverance; perseverance, character; and character, hope. And hope does not put us to shame, because God's love has been poured out into our hearts through the Holy Spirit, who has been given to us (Romans 5:3-5).

> Consider it pure joy, my brothers and sisters, whenever you face trials of many kinds, because you know that the testing of your

faith produces perseverance. Let perseverance finish its work so that you may be mature and complete, not lacking anything (James 1:2-4).

When you pass through the waters, I will be with you; and when you pass through the rivers, they will not sweep over you. When you walk through the fire, you will not be burned; the flames will not set you ablaze (Isaiah 43:2).

A good practice when we are going through a trial and feel separated from God's presence is to test our behaviors and actions through a funnel to determine where our hearts are in the midst of it. How is your time being spent? Are you prioritizing other things above your relationship with Him? Are you spending time, and I mean real time, in prayer and in His Word? I find sometimes I feel like I am spending time with the Lord when really I am just going through the motions. Is there anger and resentment toward God that the hardship is occurring in the first place?

First and foremost, we can be assured that God is always there because He said it and promised it. He says, "Never will I leave you; never will I forsake you" (Hebrews 13:5). If we look at God's track record, it's stellar; and He has never lied, so that should be enough. Unfortunately, we live in a fallen world where it's not that simple. Satan has influence in our minds, feelings, and emotions, so we battle doubt and uncertainty especially in the midst of a storm. I know that if you have lost someone close to you or are going through something heartbreaking like a divorce, it doesn't feel that easy. The truth is that it isn't. You need to compartmentalize things. One side is the feelings—let yourself grieve and feel the sorrow. The other side is being productive and walking through it with a Savior and Master who has the ability to help you through it. So how can we combat these feelings? Let's take a closer look.

We need to worship Him in the deepest way. Back to Rick Warren who says, "When you feel abandoned by God yet continue to trust him in spite of your feelings, you worship him in the deepest way."[5] This will

5. Rick Warren, *The Purpose-Driven Life,* (Grand Rapids, MI: Zondervan: 2002), 112.

not be that simple. You are combating the enemy in a way that you need to take very seriously. You have to imagine a real war that you are in. The spiritual war you are experiencing is just as real as ones that take place on earth. You need to arm yourself—protect your soul, mind, and body as though you are a soldier in that earthly war. I have experienced and seen Satan's attacks, and they are personal, vicious, and detrimental—and can take you down if you allow yourself to give in to the enemy's attack.

I understand that there are lots of emotions and feelings involved when there is suffering. Sometimes those feelings are even anger and resentment toward God for whatever the circumstance is. God can handle that if we are bringing it to Him. Even bringing anger to the cross is productive—He would rather have that than silence. I don't mean simple little "Please help me, God, I'm suffering, now fix it" prayers. I did those for years and they got me nowhere; God is not a genie or magician. I mean coming to God with the broken heart you have, bringing it to the cross, and wholeheartedly laying down your battle to Him. In the battle my family endured, I got to the point where I cried out, yelled at, and got into one-on-one intimate prayer with my Lord to help me walk through the battle because on my own I was getting nowhere. God knows what we are going through. He doesn't need to be filled in, but He needs our heart to be in the right place in order to be a part of the solution. He needs us to be open to hear what He is saying, to be willing to do what He is asking us to do, and sometimes even sacrifice things so that we can be closer to Him.

We need to dig deep and find the inner strength that is embedded deep in our souls. The verse to look at for inner strength is Ephesians 3:14-21:

> For this reason I kneel before the Father, from whom every family in heaven and on earth derives its name. I pray that out of his glorious riches he may strengthen you with power through his Spirit in your inner being, so that Christ may dwell in your hearts through faith. And I pray that you, being rooted and established in love, may have power, together with all the Lord's holy people, to grasp how wide and long and high and deep is the love of

> Christ, and to know this love that surpasses knowledge—that you may be filled to the measure of all the fullness of God. Now to him who is able to do immeasurably more than all we ask or imagine, according to his power that is at work within us, to him be glory in the church and in Christ Jesus throughout all generations, for ever and ever! Amen.

It is so important to listen to what Paul is saying as he guides us so that we develop an inner strength that can hold us through some of life's toughest storms. When I read this, the part that stands out the most to me is, "being rooted and established in love, may have power, together with all the Lord's holy people, to grasp how wide and long and high and deep is the love of Christ." Being rooted and established in His love is the key to having the inner strength God gives us to withstand the storms. To fully understand the lengths, heights, depths, and widths of God's love is the answer to having the confidence that God is with us no matter if we "feel" Him or not.

Life is not easy, objective, or manageable at many moments. We serve a God who loves us and protects us but also allows us to walk through things so we learn to rely on Him for our strength. He promises to never leave us or forsake us, but sometimes we turn our backs and try to control it all on our own. If we look at what God tells us in the Bible, it is very clear that no matter if we feel Him or not, He is with us. There are different reasons on why we feel the distance—sometimes it's our own doing and sometimes God is doing something to teach and mold us to be more like Him. If you are going through a storm where you are not feeling God with you, pour yourself into His Word like you never have before and seek Him. If you are seeking Him, He will be there and will show you why the "feeling" of distance has been there. He is always with you; don't follow what the world says and go based on your feelings—they will deceive you. Instead, trust in God's Word and His promise to always be with you.

Things to Take Away from This Chapter:

- Two times we feel distance from God:
  1. When we turn away.
  2. When He pulls away to test how we behave when we do not feel His presence.
- We have two choices when this happens:
  1. Let the enemy gain a foothold and let the situation destroy you.
  2. Protect yourself from the enemy and walk through it, fight back, and come out stronger.
- God is here no matter how I feel.
- Worship Him in the deepest way, in spite of pain and suffering.
- We don't see the big picture; there is always a lesson and a purpose in whatever we are experiencing and God will use every single aspect of it for good.
- There is an inner strength that God designed into our souls that roots us in His love and power.

Chapter 6: Know That It Is Going to Be Hard

I wish I could tell you there was a formula to make this easy for you as the spouse who stands on the other side of someone struggling. I wish I could say there were things you could do to change things or fix things and you could move on with things now perfect. That, unfortunately, is not the reality of having someone in your life who struggles with mental illness. What I can help you with is the preparation of your heart, mind, and behavior as you walk through the complex and unpredictable journey of being with someone with mental illness. This is going to be hard, please understand that. Being with someone who is struggling beyond your own relationship is so unexplainably difficult. It will come with moments of being unfair, unequal, tiring, and emotionally exhausting. There are moments when you will just want to shake them and make them snap out of it because you can see the situation from a different light, and it can be so hard when you cannot convince them otherwise. But if you keep your focus on God, He will walk with you and He will honor what you do in this battle you are enduring.

Being on the other side of the struggle is challenging and demanding. There are going to be so many moments of disappointment, let-downs, heartbreak, and tears. I believe that God can and will protect your mind and heart from certain things when you come to Him first. In my case, I know that He put a shield over my heart to protect me from the hard moments that should have truly unraveled me.

The Other Side of the Struggle

It will come with times of unfairness. Like I have said before and will say again, this is not a situation to keep a score card for what is fair and not fair. Life with someone struggling is much easier when you understand and accept that fairness is not something that will always be involved here. Life with someone who is struggling comes with many unfair moments; there are many times you are either putting more into the life that you have built together or you are taking the responsibility on yourself for something they have done. This is not something I am saying you have to accept forever, but in a harder season it may be a reality of the situation.

There will be unequal moments or even seasons of inequality. When my husband was in the thick of it, right in the height of darkness, he truly could not handle bringing much into our household, marriage, parenting, and our life. I had to take on much more responsibility than normal in these areas. The parenting category is where I noticed it the most. Helping our children get ready for the day, getting them to daycare, making dinner, and putting them to bed were, at times, completely my responsibility. It didn't last forever, but at the time it felt like it. The reality of what the struggling person is experiencing is that their struggle alone is already too much for them to handle; adding regular life on top of that is what causes the avalanche to fracture. I am not saying that you have to accept this inequality for a lifetime, but if there is something that is happening to cause them to be in a dark period, expecting equality from them is going to set you, and them, up for failure.

It can be incredibly draining. I get it—living with someone who can find the negative in almost anything is exhausting. When I was living in an enabling mindset, it actually felt easier to not be drained by it. When you try and put up boundaries and not go along for the ride into the darkness, it actually takes much more out of you. It is so important that you are being filled in other ways, because relying on the struggler's perspective to change is unrealistic and impractical.

It gets frustrating. Oh, is it ever frustrating! When you have the ability to see positive aspects of a situation, see the glass half full and be optimistic, it is so frustrating to have someone pointing out the opposite all the time. Frustration is one of the many obstacles you are almost guaranteed to come across in this role. There have been many times when I have gotten so frustrated that I decided that I was giving up. The only thing that would bring me through that is God's strength that He gives me to go on. The only way I received that strength was when I was pouring into my relationship with Him.

When I found it extremely hard was when it came to holidays or events we were committed to going to. A spiral can be triggered at any time, and it does not matter what you have planned in advance. There were smaller things like church small groups or Sunday morning church and bigger commitments like events or things you bought tickets for. Sometimes these events can be a larger stressor for the person struggling and can bring on a spiral just before you leave, which can result in them shutting down and suddenly not wanting to participate. Those were the times when I found myself getting the most worked up. It is extremely hard to be understanding and empathetic in these moments, especially when you have something to lose or if other people are depending on you both. It is hard not to bring other people into it; they will not understand why the struggling person cannot just snap out of it and continue on with the plans.

It is important to prepare yourself for things that will be thrown your way in the midst of a spiral. People who struggle tend to push people away when they need them the most; it is a characteristic of the struggle. It is the hardest concept to grasp because they act, behave, and speak in the complete opposite way. You may encounter this or you may not; in my situation, I did. There were many times when I became the victim of a verbal attack when my husband was hurting and would lash out at me. I will be honest when I say that this is one of the hardest parts of being with someone who struggles. There are no boundaries or lines they will not cross. I have heard so many times from marriage seminars to "never say this" or "never say that." I want to be clear that when dealing with mental illness, these rules do not apply to the person who is struggling when they are in a dark place. Their goal is to take the pain off of themselves and put it onto you. Their goal is to push away everything that means something because they think that maybe that is the real problem and not something within them. I can tell you that I shed many tears over the heartbreaking things that had been said to me over the years. I am not condoning or accepting it; I am not saying to tolerate it and I am not saying it is okay. But when you are with someone who struggles, it is a whole new ball game, and the rules that apply for what the world would deem a "normal" relationship just simply cannot apply here. Like I said before, it is not okay to go there—it absolutely needs to be addressed, but if the other person is not in the right headspace, you need to allow time for them to get there. It is important to prepare yourself that it likely will not be an instant conversation, but there will come a time where you know they are mentally able to handle the conversation, and at that point, it is very important to debrief the situation together. Trying to push the conversation with someone who is not ready for it usually ends in defensiveness and more chaos than if you leave it alone to die down.

When you are with someone who is struggling, pray that God gives you what I would describe as "blinders" for hurtful behavior and words. This is the only way bitterness and resentment will not plant seeds in your heart. When someone is struggling, you are, unfortunately, their safe place and person. Although that is a good thing, it also has another side to it in the sense that you are who they are going to push away and feel comfortable enough to let out their pain onto you. You don't always get the nicest behavior or words; pray that God shields your heart and mind from these things. If you dwell on those momentary behaviors, you will be taken down by the enemy. I can't explain how much God has protected me in this way, to the point that I can't even remember many situations because He has not allowed me to hold on to it one bit. Of course, you have to protect yourself and not allow yourself to get into a place where you are being abused emotionally or mentally—that is not okay, but like I said, you are their safe person so you usually get the brunt of the difficult moments. Pray for blinders to unnecessary words and protection for your heart and mind in this battle.

Another thing to prepare yourself for is how other people will respond and what they will say. People will offer advice; some will be helpful and others will be negative and discouraging. Try your best to take things with a grain of salt—they will never understand the intensity and degree of what you are dealing with or the irrationalness that encompasses the situation. I have had so many people give me advice that would never work in our situation—this is not just marital strife or arguments we are dealing with. Just remember that everyone will have an opinion and that you do not have to use anything or feel defeated by it.

I also want to tell you something and be upfront with you about your expectations of how things will go. There is no timeline you are working with. It took six very difficult years for us to even get to the point of opening Pandora's box and starting to deal with the real issues. Prior to that we were dealing with surface and symptomatic issues that were occurring. Things can get worse before they show any hope of getting better. You, unfortunately, do not get to be in charge of how and when the healing happens or how long it takes to learn how to manage what they are dealing with. You cannot force the timing to go faster, even though that may be your deepest desire.

You also cannot force someone to get help, even if you are one hundred percent sure they need it. It is like someone with an addiction—they have to want help if it is going to be successful. I remember sitting in the doctor's office and the doctor telling my husband they needed his buy-in for this to work. Sometimes it takes different medications and doses and weeks of time for medication to even work if that is the route you are taking. I remember wishing that my longing for healing could be enough to get us through that, but ultimately nothing started to change until he came to the realization himself that none of us in the situation could continue to live like that.

Take Away

Things to Take Away from This Chapter:

- It will be unfair.
- It will be unequal.
- It will be draining.
- It will be frustrating.
- God will protect you.
- Big stressors trigger big spirals.
- God can put blinders on your heart like a shield in war.
- Blinders can allow extremely hurtful situations or words to not damage you in the long run.
- Blinders cannot allow the hurt coming into your heart to turn into resentment and bitterness.
- Prepare yourself for what behaviors and words will come your way.
- Prepare yourself for what others will say and how they respond to your situation.
- Understand there is no timeline for healing; God runs the schedule, not us.
- You cannot force help on them. You need their buy-in for it to work.

Chapter 7: Take Care of Yourself

If you have ever traveled on planes, you have been instructed that in the case of the loss of cabin pressure, you need to put on your own oxygen mask before you put it on another person you are taking care of. This is the same for being on this side of the struggle. You cannot help anyone else if you are not taking care of yourself. You have to go through many of your own emotions, and it's very hard to not let those emotions get the best of you. You must take care of yourself! You cannot take care of children, a house, or be supportive to anyone else if you are not making sure you are taking care of yourself, first and foremost. It may involve getting a babysitter and going to sit in a coffee shop alone, or it may just take sitting in the bath in peace and quiet. Regardless of what you do, make it a priority. You will deteriorate if you don't.

It's important to realize that when your other half is struggling, they are not going to be able to be "the other half" and give fifty percent into even the daily parts of life. It's imbalanced, yes; it's unfortunate, yes; but if allowing them to take some things off their plate helps them overcome their battle, then in the end it will be worth it.

When we were in the midst of our biggest battle, an everyday thing like getting the kids ready for daycare was such a monumental task for my husband that it really was too much for him to handle at that time in his life. I know many people wouldn't understand this and would say that I should've expected him to be able to parent with me. But I knew the realities of it, and if it meant for a time that I allowed him to focus on getting himself better and I got the kids ready for daycare, I will always come back to the fact that, in the end, his well-being was more important. In order for me not to fall apart, the key was finding new ways to make sure I was doing okay during this time. I took up people's offers to have my kids over to play, I went to a counselor and made sure I was able to process what was going on, and I made sure I was reaching out to people to have them pray with me. I truly felt like I was being filled up in all the ways I needed to be in order to deal with the magnitude of the situation. The amazing thing is that now that the battle is over and because I took this approach during the struggle, my husband is eager and willing to help get the kids ready without me having to nag or hassle!

You need to look at what you can do for yourself to get through the complex situation of having a spouse who struggles with mental illness. The point of this is to make sure that when the other person is falling apart, you don't fall apart with them. So how can you do this?

Allow yourself to feel. Being strong all the time is not reasonable or even possible. We are emotional beings and if we push those feelings down, they will become repressed and pop back up later in life or in unhealthy ways. We need to allow ourselves to be frustrated, to be angry, to be drained, to be sad, to be desperate, and even to be hopeless. When we come to God saying, "I can't do this anymore," we are in the place He actually needs us to be. I say this because we are not the ones doing anything to make change happen. It's all in God's power, not ours. So allow yourself to feel the emotions you are experiencing, but this is the important part—do not dwell on them! Feel them, grieve them, then leave them at the cross and let God start working.

Your Support Team

You need a team who can hold you up at times when you may not be able to stand. Prayer warriors are one of the most indispensable teams you can have on your side. Your church family is an extension of God's love. You need that support just as much as your spouse needs your support. Your spouse cannot offer you the support you need, but there are so many people God will place in your life to fill in the support. Do not pass them up; you are not strong enough to go through it alone—that is not how we were designed.

It is okay to accept help. There are no rewards for doing this by yourself. There is no weakness in accepting help when people offer it. Our human nature is to help when someone is struggling, so if friends or family are offering, I urge you to take them up on it. If people are offering to bring you meals, to watch the children while you have a moment alone, to have you over for coffee, don't pass that up. The world continuously teaches us that we need to be strong all the time, that we cannot lean on others because everything is focused on "me, me, me," and this mentality can actually make us think we are inadequate because we accept help. This simply is not true; you will fall apart if you try and keep quiet and do this on your own. Something will break—and it will likely be you.

Finding an outlet that is yours and yours alone is crucial for you so you don't get taken down with the struggling person. Don't give up on your own hobbies or activities because those things can give you the perfect break and a way to release the stress that comes with being with someone who struggles. For me, it became writing, but it can be anything—anything that is solely focused on you. This is the area to be selfish in! Exercise is great because it helps you physically as well as mentally. It can be something that becomes part of your routine, or sometimes it may be an hour at a coffee shop alone because things are escalating and you need some time away from it all.

Don't be afraid to seek out any type of counseling yourself. I would highly recommend a Christian counselor because, from my experience, people who live "of the world" have a very different opinion of how you should act and would encourage you to walk away from that person a lot quicker than someone who values the commitment of marriage. Professional help can provide an objective viewpoint but also guide you through the journey and provide you with coping skills that you need to get through without picking up any negative coping mechanisms that you may unintentionally use. In many towns there is a mental health resource center that may have either programs, counselors, or at least books that can help you work through your own emotions while reading through them.

Do not let it get personal. It is important to not take the behavior, or even the words, of the struggling person personally, even when it very much feels and looks personal. Learning as much as you can about what you are dealing with can help you compartmentalize the mental illness away from the person, allowing you to see that it is not an attack on you but a cry for help to you if they turn on you with their words or behavior.

Take Away

Things to Take Away from This Chapter:

- You cannot help anyone if you do not help yourself first.
- Allow yourself to feel.
- Seek professional help if you need to.
- Find your own outlet.
- Look for support systems all around you.
- Never be afraid to accept help.

Chapter 8: Be Held

My daughter fell off the couch the other day and hit her head (lightly); I jumped up and grabbed her and held her tight to me. I couldn't do anything to stop the pain, I couldn't change the circumstances, but I could hold her through it. It brought me back to a song that came to me during a very challenging time when God was saying to me, "Just let Me hold you through this."

Sometimes with the busyness of life and with us trying to control everything we struggle just being still, we struggle letting God hold us like the father He is. Our culture is pushing swiftness and impulsive behavior; being still is becoming more and more of a foreign concept to us. Life presents obstacles that we can't understand, that we, in all reality, can't control, although we try anyway. Many times in these experiences God is asking us to stop, be held, and allow Him to work. If we look at when Jesus was here on earth and doing His ministry, we see how important being still with God was to Him. It took precedence over everything else and was treated as sacred time. I don't know about you, but when I try being still I have a very hard time doing it and letting go of the control. It is something that is a learned skill and very foreign in our culture today.

If you are in the middle of the storm, allow yourself to be held by God. Don't worry about always being strong; let your God wrap His arms around you and hold you in the hard moments. Be open to the people and circumstances He will put in your path to allow that holding to extend into tangible ways of seeing it happening. We are going to see what it looks like to be held by God on this earth because it is not always easy to see.

The Other Side of the Struggle

I firmly believe that God uses people to help people. We are all the vessels He uses to show and be His love. During the most difficult and stressful times in my life, God brought people into my path or had people who were already there step up when I needed them the most. Keep your eyes peeled for them; they are your blessing! It can be in forms of bringing you meals, babysitting your children while you get a moment of rest, a friend to talk to, or a shoulder to cry on. It may show up as a person to give you advice or just to keep you from exploding. These people are not a coincidence; they are sent and they are purposeful. Don't pass up what they are there to offer; they are a godsend to you and can give you the strength to endure the storm.

Just like we talked about with taking care of ourselves, finding a channel that God has personally designed to build us and fill us up that is only ours is another way God holds us. He designed us; He created these interests and passions that are personal to use for times like these. Whatever it is, it is only for you because it was created for you; it will not help the person next to you in a hard time. This is how much He loves us—He ingrained these passions inside of us so we can utilize them when we are in need. The world offers us other temporary fixes like alcohol, drugs, or indulging in things that on the surface may seem like they help, but in reality they are hurting us and taking us away from God.

For myself, reading and writing became a way that I connected to God in really difficult times. If you don't intentionally have purposeful outlets, you are in danger of picking up unhealthy ones like addictions or traps of the enemy. Be on guard about this. Maybe it's exercise or coloring— it doesn't matter, but it will be personal and unique to you and you alone and it will build you up, which is why God designed it that way for you. Be on guard and make sure you are prioritizing a healthy outlet for yourself if you are in the middle of one of life's storms. If you don't, the enemy will gain a foothold and make his own coping mechanisms for you, which will only have your demise as the end goal.

Another way you come into Jesus's arms is by bringing your struggle to the cross; cry out, yell, bring your frustration, bring your pain—God can handle it. Bring it all to the only One who can do anything with it.

The world can only bring you so far, and it's usually further away from God. The world can offer you quick fixes, bandage solutions, and an unsatisfying answer to the problem. The true, lasting, and real solution to any problem and any storm is only through the power of God. My best advice for getting through any storm is get down on those knees of yours and lay it all out there. God has power to change a heartbreaking situation into a miracle in incomprehensible ways that we cannot do on our own strength. The battle we have in doing this is in giving over the control—it's a struggle for our sinful heart. Prepare yourself for this power struggle because the world has taught us that our strength comes from being able to do it on our own. That is a downright lie—we cannot do it without the supernatural strength of Jesus, and we need to continually remind ourselves of that. Be prepared to give it to God, only to realize you are still holding on with your pinky finger. It is such an incredibly hard thing to let go of something you so desperately want to control yourself, but that is not how God works.

We need to switch our gaze from the storm and onto Jesus. I continuously have to take my thoughts captive with this notion. Where am I fixing my eyes? What am I focusing on? Am I dwelling on the storm and doubting God's ability or am I trusting that I believe He can bring victory to it? Am I saying I believe with my words but my heart is questioning it? When we switch our focus off of the negative situation we are enduring and refocus it onto Christ, it changes everything. It gives us hope, it gives us clarity, it gives us strength. When we focus on the storm we feel defeated—we feel the darkness and hopelessness and mentally, emotionally, and physically give up. Take your thoughts captive, keep your mind continuously aware of what your focus is on, and keep bringing it back to God and His Word.

I want to encourage anyone reading this that no matter your storm—whether it's big or small—you can endure it. I know firsthand how much it *feels* like you can't, like it is going to overtake you and your life is about to collapse. I plead with you to reach out and find the areas that God is giving you to be held in this storm. I can assure you they are there but not always easy to see if you are focused on the storm.

Take Away

Things to Take Away from This Chapter:

- God uses people to help people.
- God designed specific vehicles for you to be filled up and to feel loved.
- Get on your knees and lay it all out to Him there.
- Switch your gaze.

Chapter 9: Know the Truth

C hances are, there are a lot of good things about your spouse—that is why you fell in love and married them. If it is a family member or close friend, you know there are countless good aspects to them and that this illness does not define who they truly are even though it can be hard to see that side at times. Things get very clouded when things get dark; it is hard to see the good, let alone focus on it. It is important that the good aspects do not get overtaken by the negative moments.

I read something that changed my life: "Never doubt in the dark what God told you in the light." It is such a powerful statement. If you know the truth in the light, you cannot allow the darkness to cause you to waver from it. That is exactly the enemy's goal, and we cannot let him win that. It is important that we constantly remind ourselves of the truth— the truth of the person who is struggling, the truth about ourselves and our own strength to get through the dark times, and most importantly the truth of God and His promises.

"Truth journaling" is something I would consider trying out to help you during the hard moments. The key is to write it when you are in a good place and read it when you are not. Buy yourself a journal, write it on the computer—it doesn't matter where it is, but when you are in a good headspace write out a list of truths. Truths about your spouse when they are at their best. Truths about God. This can be very helpful. When things start going in a direction that isn't so positive, you can pull those out and focus on them. I would recommend putting them somewhere you will come across pretty easily, as it is not going to be the first thing you feel like doing when things are hard. When you are frustrated or angry, it is really difficult to convince yourself to read a positive list about that struggling person or pray for them. I find if it is somewhere like on the wall beside my bed, I will end up looking at it at some point and be reminded that I need to sit down and read it.

Not only is it important to look at the truths about your spouse, but it is important to look at God's truths—what He tells us and also who He is. Let's take a moment and look at God's goals and characteristics and what His truths are that He tells us in the Bible.

> The Lord himself goes before you and will be with you; he will never leave you nor forsake you. Do not be afraid; do not be discouraged (Deuteronomy 31:8).

> The Lord is my helper; I will not be afraid; what can mere mortals do to me? (Hebrews 13:6)

> And we know that in all things God works for the good of those who love him, who have been called according to his purpose (Romans 8:28).

> When you pass through the waters, I will be with you; and when you pass through the rivers, they will not sweep over you. When you walk through the fire, you will not be burned; the flames will not set you ablaze (Isaiah 43:2).

These are some examples of who God is, this is what the Bible teaches us, and even when we go through tough times these truths do not change. These are promises He gives us for those times we doubt His loyalty and dedication to what He said to us in the Bible.

Something to know about this process is that when things start getting cloudy, Satan will do everything in his power to stop you from even opening it up. He gains more power when he feeds you lies about this person, he gains more power when he keeps you angry and resentful, and he loves bitterness and offense. So prepare yourself that you will not be jumping for joy and eager to reach for that truth list. You must do it more out of an obedient heart, saying to God, "I trust that Your truth is far beyond anything I can fabricate, and I choose to read this list and focus on the good and allow You to soften my heart in this situation."

Praying for the other person is another mission you should have when they go into the darkness. It will not be easy; I have said many unenthusiastic prayers while gritting my teeth. Praying for the struggling person allows God to come into your heart and soften it. If there is anger there, this will seem very difficult to do, but if you can start teaching yourself to pray first—before you allow yourself to get upset and go down a rabbit trail of why this person is so terrible—you will be amazed how God can change the outcome of a situation. An encouraging point is that the closer you grow in your relationship with God, the quicker you will get to this place. I remember the first time I told myself that I would pray for my husband when I was angry—it took an entire evening to even start! But as I have built up my relationship with God, now prayer is sometimes the first thing that comes to my mind when I am upset.

I was recently at a small group and my husband did not show up after work because he was having a rough day. I was so angry! I had both kids with me and they were being very "hands on" and I was exhausted. I just wanted a second pair of hands to help with the kids and I also wanted to share the learning with him. I am a very impulsive person, which usually gets me in trouble in these situations because I tend to say things quickly and without thinking and end up making the situation worse. I sat there and kept sending text messages to him, but because I was praying as I was doing this, I keep erasing the mean texts one after another. I knew that sending a mean message would only push him further into the darkness, would create a huge fight when I got home, and, in reality, I was not being very understanding of where his headspace was in the first place for not showing up. It was amazing—I probably had written over five mean messages that I never sent because God kept telling me to stop. I ended up going home, and although it wasn't all great right away, slowly the evening turned around. Had I sent even one of those texts, the entire night would have been completely different and probably would have ended with much worse things spoken. Because I have trained myself over the years to run to God first, He gives me opportunities to make the choice of either softening my heart or falling into the traps of Satan with negative results.

Take Away

Things to Take Away from This Chapter:

- Never doubt in the dark what God told you in the light.
- Truth journaling:
  - Truths about the other person
  - Truths about God
- Know that Satan will always try and cloud the truth with his evil.
- Pray for them in the hardest moments and allow God to work within your heart and see the changes that can be made when you bring a softened heart into a situation.

Chapter 10: Boundaries

I said in the beginning of the book that abusive behavior is never okay, no matter how dark of a place a person may be. You can never tolerate it because the moment you do it takes on a life of its own and it is very hard to stop enabling the behavior and excusing the abuse. When someone is struggling with some dark issues, their biggest defense is to push you away. The way that happens is by lashing out at you with very hurtful words. We all do this to a degree when we are upset, but in my experience people dealing with mental illness take this "lashing out" defense a step further. You have to draw a personal line for yourself and commit to not allow a situation to go past that line. You need to set clear boundaries for your spouse and stick to them. You cannot let yourself get into a position of abuse, and if you are there already you need to seek counsel outside your friends and family and find a professional who can guide you in that situation.

What we are talking about here is how you are going to protect yourself, your heart, your mind, and your family. You have to decide where your personal line is, where tolerable behavior ends, and when you have to stop things from going to an unacceptable place. It is about standing up for yourself and finding the balance between support and the border where behavior will no longer be permitted. Just because you are a supportive person to someone who is struggling doesn't give them the right to treat you wrong or make you a doormat. Boundaries help define the margins for everyone to know where it is safe to be and where stepping out of bounds is.

I used to have zero boundaries with my husband, and it turned into a very negative situation not only for me but our entire family. When my husband would have a spiral I would allow him to speak negatively and lash out, usually at me and my emotions. I would even tell him to go out and do something he loved (like climbing or golfing) and basically reward him for emotionally attacking me. When he came back into a good headspace, he would apologize and we would move on from the situation. The problem was that by brushing it off, I was allowing this behavior to continue and showing him that it was okay to treat me poorly whenever he was in a bad headspace. What's worse, I was showing my children it was okay for people to say whatever they want when they were upset as long as they apologized after.

The scariest part about all of this is that I had no idea I was doing it! I was convinced that I was being a supportive and amazing wife by doing it. It was not until I was explaining it to a family member and I saw the horror on their face that I realized that this was not a healthy way to be dealing with things. It wasn't until I stepped back a bit from the situation to see what was going on. Once I did, I could not even believe how it had gotten to that point, but it helped me to learn much more about boundaries, how to have them, and how to bring them into a boundary-less relationship.

Now I have created boundaries. I have personal rules for myself that do not allow this to happen anymore. I cannot control my husband's behavior when he gets into a bad headspace, but what I can do is control what I will accept coming my way. Although he may not be able to control the way he is acting, that doesn't mean the abusive or hurtful behavior can just continue. When you are first creating your boundaries, you need to communicate these with the other person when they are in a good frame of mind so they do not feel completely smacked in the face when you try to implement them during a hard time. This is something that is very important to communicate in a good headspace as you try and walk the journey of finding boundaries. Some key things you need to communicate are:

- You love them.
- You are not walking away, even though they may feel that's what the boundaries are.

- You are not giving up on them, but it's okay to protect yourself.

- You are supporting them by using boundaries.

One of the biggest things I have learned is if he says anything that effects me personally, I will then start to engage and metaphorically "fuel the fire." When I react and give in to the emotions that he is trying to stir up in me, it causes him to put the issues on me, not himself and his problems in the situation. The best thing I can do is remove myself from being around him if he is not going to speak to me nicely. Because I told him about this before his state of mind was troubled, it wasn't a shock when I did do it, and even though he may not like it while it's happening, he knows the reason behind it. This way he knows that I am not walking away and abandoning him but putting up limitations around what is acceptable and where the line gets crossed.

The key to boundaries is to understand that they are a form of love and protection for you both. If you look at your children, we put boundaries in their lives to keep them safe. If we allowed them to run in the middle of the road they could get hurt; it is the same concept here. If we do not have borders that the struggling person cannot cross, everyone ends up hurt. Keep reminding yourself that boundaries are love because if you are trying to bring them into a situation where you have lived without them, they will likely not be well received at first. Not only are boundaries good for the other person, they are good for you too. They protect you in the situation just as much as the other person. Like I said before, you can only control yourself, so implementing boundaries within the relationship is just as important. I will share some boundaries that we have found successful in our situation.

Remove Myself

Walking away is the best way to defuse a situation. I am not saying to be disrespectful to your spouse and walk away just because you don't like what you are hearing. But it is okay when it becomes disrespectful and harmful to you and the relationship to walk away until things settle down. It is not okay to be spoken to negatively or for them to hurt you with their words, and if walking away is the only way to stop that, you need to do it. Once things start getting disrespectful, it is my responsibility to walk away and not tolerate it to any degree.

No Enabling

I learned that I cannot give my husband compensation for behaving in a negative way toward me or excuse that type of behavior because of the struggle. Many times things can get swept under the umbrella of the struggle, but once it becomes hurtful, that is where you need to draw the line and stick to it.

Be Consistent

If one day you are tolerating hurtful words and the next you are not, it won't go over well in the long run. If you draw a line in the sand, do not accept that line being crossed even one time. Eventually, they will learn you are serious and start respecting the boundary you have created.

Boundaries Are Not Ultimatums

Setting boundaries does not mean you withhold things if the other person does not comply. It is caring enough about yourself to not be taken down with them and also loving them enough to put limits on where they can go with you. Boundaries are not you saying, "If you do this, you will not get (or you will lose) this," or threatening to leave them.

Not Ignoring the Problem If Boundaries Get Crossed

If you have clearly made a border line that gets crossed, you need to follow through with the aftermath of that, or else there is no point to have the boundary in place to begin with. Like I said, you don't deal with them in an ultimatum sense, but there needs to be a conversation and an understanding that it happened and that it cannot happen again.

Take Away

Things to Take Away from This Chapter:

- Abuse is never okay and never to be tolerated.
- Boundaries are critical for both yourself and the struggler.
- Boundaries are love and protection for both sides of the situation.
- In a good headspace, explain to them what your boundaries are in a loving way. Although they may not like them in a bad headspace, they will at least know why you are putting them up.
- Know that you can only control yourself in the situation; that is what you need to focus on.
- Remove yourself from the situation.
- Be consistent.
- Do not allow enabling to creep in.
- Boundaries do not entail ultimatums.
- If the boundaries are crossed it must be addressed and dealt with.

Chapter 11: Enabling versus Supporting

This is something that took me years to learn. For six years I thought I was being the supportive wife who was walking a difficult road with my husband; only after I stepped back from the situation was I able to see that I had become an enabler to my husband's poor behavior when he was in a bad headspace. What I was really doing was hurting both of us by allowing the dysfunction to continue. There is a fine line between enabling and supporting, and you need to understand the difference between them. Like I mentioned earlier, I crossed that line without even knowing it. When my husband would go into a spiral, I would be so desperate for it to end that I knew sending him to do an activity he loved would possibly snap him out of it. Unfortunately, what this created was an environment where he would be rewarded, in a sense, for treating me poorly.

There is a fine line between self-care and enabling. Sometimes the best thing for my husband is for him to get away and clear his head by doing something he is passionate about. One of the hardest things is trying to figure out where it is crossing the line from good for their well-being into an enabling behavior on your end. I admit that we have not yet found that balance, but because I am now aware that enabling is a real possibility and used to be my default behavior, I can evaluate the situation and see if I am being supportive or enabling. It is also great because I have a wonderful team in place that I can bounce ideas off of; if I tell them about a situation and they see a red flag, they will immediately bring it to my attention. This type of support team is very important because you are so close to the situation that your focus is too narrow and honed in on the moments as they happen that you cannot identify when you are falling into your default modes. This is another reason why I keep reiterating that you need other people who are safe places for you to confide in who will not be afraid to step in and tell you when you are participating in the situation in ways like enabling.

Let's analyze the difference between enabling, helping, and supporting someone who is struggling. First we will explore the definitions of these three words.

Enable

To make able, give power, means, or ability to;

To make possible or easy.[6]

Support

To sustain or withstand without giving way.

To undergo or endure, especially with patience or submission; tolerate.

To sustain under trial or affliction.

To maintain by supplying with things necessary to existence; provide for.

To uphold by aid, countenance, one's vote, etc.; back; second.[7]

Help

To give or provide what is necessary to accomplish a task or satisfy a need; contribute strength or means to; render assistance to; cooperate effectively with; aid; assist.

To save; rescue; succor.

To make easier or less difficult; contribute to; facilitate.

To be useful or profitable to.

To relieve (someone) in need or distress.[8]

---

6. Dictionary.com Unabridged, s.v. "enable," Random House, Inc., http://www.dictionary.com/browse/enable (accessed: June 7, 2017).

7. Dictionary.com Unabridged, s.v. "support," Random House, Inc., http://www.dictionary.com/browse/support (accessed: June 7, 2017).

8. Dictionary.com Unabridged, s.v. "help," Random House, Inc., http://www.dictionary.com/browse/help (accessed: June 7, 2017).

In summary, helping is doing something for someone else that they are unable to do for themselves, whereas enabling is doing things for someone else that they *can* and *should* be doing for themselves and/or making excuses for their behavior, which in turn allows them to continue the behavior. They look very different when you see what they actually mean. Supporting and helping are comprised of words like *assist, relieve, sustain,* and *patience,* while enabling involves words like *allow, let,* and *permit.*

Enabling gets confused with help and support because the intentions for all of them are well-meant. Enabling never comes from a destructive or harmful heart, but a heart that is so desperate for the dark time to pass and a way to protect themselves from the effects if they were to combat against the behavior. Enabling can prolong or intensify dysfunctional behavior, even if it is coming from a good place.

Enabling usually creates a co-dependent relationship. Codependents often feel required to solve other people's problems but then become dependent on the other person's struggle themselves. Our human nature is to problem solve and fix things; when dealing with someone with mental illness, it is extremely hard to grasp the concept that we are not able to fix the other person. We are so close to this person; we love them and we know their heart. We don't want to believe this continuous behavior is intentional, so we are convinced that it will stop if we move on from it. Once the chaos of the episode is over, we are so exhausted and drained from it that we just want to get to a happier place. Dwelling in it keeps reminding you of what happened so it is easier to forgive and move on; but sometimes we don't allow the proper amount of time for remorse and apologizing to show that the behavior is not acceptable— then it turns into enabling. It is also easier to not "rock the boat" and go back into a bad headspace so we move on; but again, this shows that negative behavior is acceptable and can happen again. We also want to maintain our own appearance to people in our lives, so it becomes a cycle of covering the behavior and trying to not dwell on it when it does happen so we can go back to living life normally.

The Other Side of the Struggle

Here are some questions to ask yourself if you have someone in your life struggling. If you answer yes to most of the questions, you may have crossed over from supportive to enabling.

- Do you often overlook or discount unacceptable behavior?
- Do you find yourself feeling bitter about the tasks and duties you take on?
- Do you consistently put your own needs and desires last to put the other persons first?
- Do you have anxiety about communicating your own emotions?
- Do you ever feel worried that not doing something will cause a major problem?
- Do you ever lie to cover for someone else's behavior?
- Do you continue to offer help when it is never valued or respected?

Usually when talking about enabling it is in reference to addictions. Something important to realize is that the darkness that comes to a person struggling with mental illness becomes somewhat comfortable to them. I am not necessarily saying that they are addicted to struggling, but once you live in a certain condition for a long time it becomes predictable and secure. When someone lives in darkness, the light becomes a scary and unstable place. It may seem backward to someone who is always in a good frame of mind, but for someone who wrestles with mental illness, this is a very good description of how they live. There are many theories that actually do believe that darkness becomes addictive to a person. Having lived through it myself, there are many areas that addiction and mental illness cross over.

After the Spiral

Another area to look at is what happens when the spiral or episode is over. How to deal with the aftermath of the spiral is an art—one I am no expert in by any means, but I have tried every way possible and have found ways that work and ones that backfire and hurt me in the end.

How do you move on without dwelling on what happened for too long, and at the same time truly forgiving so bitterness and resentment do not build in your heart? This, my friends, is a tough one and takes a lot of work to accomplish.

Sometimes when a person is coming back down from a spiral it is not quick and they are not remorseful right away. I view a spiral as an altered state of mind, so it reminds me of coming down off of a "high" in some comparisons. If you push too hard as they are coming down, there is a chance you will push them right back into the spiral. I tend to do this a lot, and it creates headache and stress for me more than anyone else. During a spiral, there were likely a lot of either not so nice words or behavior that were said and done, and you need to now deal with the repercussions of that. I have learned that forcing an apology right away usually gets a very insincere and artificial apology, which ends up making me more upset. I understand that they may have done many things that were wrong, and to just forgive them without an apology seems ludicrous. The secret is that I need to let my husband come down completely before even attempting the apology route.

What I have also learned is that forgiveness is not based on his remorse over the situation, but it's not okay to allow them to think that hurtful behavior directed toward you is acceptable. At the same time, if you do not deal with the situation and just move on, that is another form of enabling. This is why I say there is a fine balance. I find this part dependent on the situation. Some are more serious and the hurt is much greater so we need to spend more time focusing on the repentance of it. Some situations can move forward after a simple apology. We all have different needs for the types of apologies we need to move on from a situation. It can be helpful to learn what you need and communicate that to them so at least they know what you need to move on.

Take Away

Things to Take Away from This Chapter:

- Differentiate between being supportive and enabling.

- There is a difference between enabling and allowing self-care; finding that line can be tricky.

- Enabling is doing things for someone else that they *can* and *should* be doing for themselves and/ or making excuses for their behavior, which in turn allows them to continue the behavior.

- Supporting and helping mean doing something for someone else that they are unable to do for themselves, holding someone up when they are unable to hold themselves up.

- Enabling usually creates co-dependent relationship. Co-dependents often feel required to solve other people's problems but then become dependent on the other person's struggle themselves.

- Once a spiral or episode is over, it needs to be dealt with in a healthy way because enabling tendencies can creep up here as well.

- Living in darkness for a long time can create a predictable and safe environment, and the light can become a scary and unnerving place for them.

Chapter 12: You Can't Counsel Your Spouse

Early on in our marriage someone gave me this wonderful piece of advice: "You can't counsel your spouse," and it has always stuck in the back of my head. It doesn't matter if you have read every book on the subject, you will not be the one to fix this situation. Accept that now. If you want to get the award for fixing your spouse, then realize it will cost you your relationship. It's the hardest thing to do, but stepping back and letting God work is the only real and lasting solution. The more you meddle, the less real work can get done. You are standing in the way and actually become an obstacle the more you try to intervene. There are small areas where you can have a participatory role, so do not get discouraged by this notion. Just know that mental illness is bigger than you, and as a spouse you are too close to the situation to be the one to fix it. Our role can be many things; it can be supportive, empathetic, understanding, accommodating, compassionate, reassuring, and entail many more positions that are needed for the success of the situation.

My husband came with a past just like every person on this planet. His past was entangled with lies from the enemy. One lie told him that he tried to get help once and it didn't work. For years, I accepted that. I thought we could get through this with enough love and support, but sometimes that truly isn't enough. I learned that those lies I mentioned, the ones from his past, were being used by Satan like dodge balls against my husband, keeping him down and not even daring to come out. He was being pummeled by these lies. While this was happening intervention was necessary, but here is the key: It will not be from you. You are too close, to familiar, too devoted, and you involving yourself in this part of the process can be detrimental to the relationship in the long run. You have to be open and okay that someone else may speak into this situation and it will be better received from them. If you love this person, them coming out of the darkness needs to be more important than you being the hero bringing them out.

If someone close to you is battling something bigger than themselves, you cannot mend all the broken pieces on your own. As humans we are problem solvers, we want to fix people—especially when they are broken, and especially when it is someone you love. The reality is that you just can't. Even if you are qualified in the area, you are too close to it, too emotionally involved, and for the majority of us we truly are not qualified. Even doctors have rules about having their family members as patients, even when it comes to surgeries. We need to look at it like that—we are too partial to this person and we do not have the ability to look at the situation objectively enough.

Just because you cannot counsel your spouse does not mean you do not need your own counsel. I am a big fan of counseling, but then again I am a women and love to talk, especially talking about my feelings, so I am likely biased. I do believe talking to an objective party can be extremely beneficial. They see things you don't see; they see how both of you are behaving. The sad truth is, you are not perfect and you are an emotional being, and chances are you are doing things that are not advantageous to the situation.

As you try and step back from fixing your spouse on your own, make sure you have some safe people for you to talk to. I had an amazing and divinely positioned friend at the time who was a counselor. She was able to show me that this was beyond me and that this was not going to just get better on its own.

More importantly, make sure the people you are confiding in are the right people. Especially if this is an area that does not need to be public information, which these things do not tend to be. We had an agreement—my husband knew that I am a female and need to talk, so we made an agreement that allowed me to confide in certain people whom he trusted to provide safe and sound council to me during this time in our lives. I didn't want to disrespect him or betray his trust, but I also needed support in this very difficult time. This was a way that we found worked for us as he approved this small circle of people whom I could go to for help without airing all our problems to the world or letting our problems get into the wrong hands.

Each person in this world is different, each diagnosis is different and each environment that illness is living in is unique, so I cannot speak into any situation other than mine. If you feel that there is a need for outside and/or professional help, there are many ways to get that. What I do know is that each situation does not have to get as ugly as ours did before reaching out for help. Some people are willing to get help, others are neutral, and others are against it completely. That piece of the puzzle is extremely important because the success of the help lies in that. You need the other person's "buy in" to gain any movement because anything forced will backfire in your face. Yet at the same time, if they truly do need help and won't get it, that is a very hard place to be. I know because I lived that way for years.

In short, trying to involve yourself in the "restoration" of things usually will make things worse. Your role needs to be the supporter, not the fixer. God is the ultimate Restoration Master, and you need to get to a place where you can listen and obey to find out how God is going to work in your situation. There are ways He will use you and your presence, but it must be guided by His direction. Pray about how God wants you to approach the situation. Maybe you do all the research and find what is in your immediate area and can present that to the struggling person in a loving way, and that will make them consider getting help. Maybe God will reveal another person He wants to be the messenger of that information, and that is okay. Many times people listen better to people other than their spouse.

Take Away

Things to Take Away from This Chapter:

- You are not qualified to counsel your spouse.
- Reaching out to a safe person is helpful to you.
- Utilizing professional counseling; they should be the only one qualified to help in a therapeutic capacity.

Chapter 13: Unconditional Love

If the struggling person is your spouse, when you committed to marriage you committed to "for better or worse." Well my friend, this is the worse! We live in a society that tells you it's okay to jump ship at this stage of the game, but it's not. Dig deep, because it won't be easy, but stick it out and don't give up. Your spouse needs your unconditional love more than ever right now, so give it freely and without expectation of anything back in return—they likely can't give you that right now. Go to God for your source of love, hope, and strength because that is the only way you will get what you need in this difficult time.

If you have children, you have a better understanding of this concept. You know there is nothing they could do that would make you stop loving them. They likely do things all the time that make you angry, frustrated, and even disappointed. You may even go through moments of not liking what they are doing, but that does not change the love you have for them. Now look at your spouse. Do they feel that way about your love for them? This question caught my attention the first time I heard it. There are moments that I can honestly say no. My husband probably questioned me at times because my actions did not convey that. My deepest goal is that when my husband looks back on even the darkest of times, he will see unwavering, steadfast, and unfaltering love from me.

See, we as adults have been tainted by the world—by our upbringings, our experiences, by mistakes, and by sin. We see marriages fall apart everywhere we look. It's hard to find true examples of unconditional love these days, but if our goal is to strive to have a marriage that makes it to the end—the type of marriage God designed marriage to be—we have to find it and make sure it shows. More importantly, we need our spouses to know that regardless of all the arguments, disagreements, and different points of view that come with living with another person, there is nothing the enemy can do that will make you give up.

Unconditional love is love without limitations and without conditions; it is complete love. But unconditionally loving someone doesn't mean being subject to abuse or letting yourself be walked all over like a doormat. Please don't confuse these things; if you are not being treated right, seek help outside of your marriage to find the proper solution. What it *does* mean, though, is that you will not give up when it gets hard. It means you will forgive; it means you will work through your issues; it means that no matter what obstacles, curveballs, and problems life throws at your relationship you will commit to coming out stronger and not letting it tear you apart. That seems like a large task, doesn't it?

So what is unconditional love, and how do we display this in our marriage?

Understand you will not always "like" your spouse. Love and like are two very different things. There are many times, I can tell you, when I don't like my husband, his actions, or something he said. I know for a fact he can say that about me, and I am sure any couple can say that about their spouse as well. Does that mean I don't support him? Absolutely not. I would do anything for my husband, even though he doesn't always make me "happy" every moment. Happiness is a feeling, and feelings can lead you to some very dark places. Love is bigger than like, and you can love someone wholeheartedly and still have moments of not liking their behavior.

Unconditional love means walking through difficult situations and coming out stronger than you went in.If your truly meant the vows you said to your spouse on your wedding day, then you will find a way to overcome the storms of life. I get it—they can be hard and they can make you feel like you don't want to overcome them. But unconditional love truly means being able to look at the bigger picture and working through it even when you're not "feeling it."

Loving someone unconditionally also means not allowing your feelings rule the situation. Feelings are deceiving, they lie to you, they are moment by moment. But they are strong, they are convincing, and they can really guide your actions if you let them. Feelings are in the moment; unconditional love is the big picture.

We have to make sure that we don't hold on to the past. Holding grudges, resentment, and bitterness is the complete opposite of unconditional love. They actually stand in the way for unconditional love to grow; we need to forgive, forgive, forgive! Moving forward and realizing that your relationship is more important than you being right or winning an argument is the essence of unconditionally loving your spouse.

You have to watch your expectations. Love them without having expectations of the outcome, of your spouse, and of getting anything in return. This is very difficult for us with our sinful nature.

Never give up. Life is tough. As you live life with another person, you will come up against different opinions, struggles, temptations, and much more. If you are loving your spouse unconditionally, you are committed and not walking away when things get rough.

In all honesty, I believe if you want a lasting relationship, unconditional love needs to be present and at the core of your marriage. If it's not, life's storms will knock you around and allow you to make decisions that are based on feelings, and those decisions will destroy you when they doesn't need to. The world teaches us differently. It tells us that love can be temporary and that we should end it once it starts getting hard. It tells us that once the "feeling" of love is gone, we should walk away and try and find it somewhere else. The truth is that once the feelings leave, that is where true love begins to grow. Unconditional love is persistent and dedicated love; it is the love Jesus has for us. He is our role model to emulate and follow when we try and express this type of love to others. This is the love Jesus talked about throughout His entire ministry. There are different types of love that Jesus teaches us about in the Bible. The only way to understand how we can display unconditional love is to look at Jesus's example.

The Other Side of the Struggle

Your love, Lord, reaches to the heavens, your faithfulness to the skies (Psalms 36:5).

The Lord appeared to us in the past, saying: "I have loved you with an everlasting love; I have drawn you with unfailing kindness" (Jeremiah 31:3).

Love is patient, love is kind. It does not envy, it does not boast, it is not proud. It does not dishonor others, it is not self-seeking, it is not easily angered, it keeps no record of wrongs. Love does not delight in evil but rejoices with the truth. It always protects, always trusts, always hopes, always perseveres (1 Corinthians 13:4-7).

God's love is constant, everlasting, unfailing, kind, and unending. The only way we can display this to others is to fall back on what God has taught us about this love He designed. This is not always a natural feeling because we have sin nature in our beings and we are combating a world that tells us that everything is all about us. This inward focus is the opposite of the love Jesus teaches us about. It tells us that we don't have to love someone for better and for worse, but that we can simply walk away once it becomes unpleasant. God created us with this love for a reason, and the world has twisted this into this new model of love that is dispensable and replaceable; that is not the truth. The world may tell you it is okay to jump ship, but God is asking you to walk through it and lean on Him as you do, and He honors that and rewards us when we do. I can promise you this—if you take the unconditional love approach you will always walk out the other side stronger. God will use every part of the journey for His good, but the key is that you have to get there.

Take Away

Things to Take Away from This Chapter:

- Unconditional love is what we are called to do.
- Unconditional love has no strings attached.
- Unconditionally loving someone doesn't mean abuse or allowing yourself to be walked all over or be a doormat.
- Understand you will not always "like" your spouse. Love and like are very different things.
- Walk through difficult situations and you will come out stronger than you went in.
- Don't allow your feelings rule the situation.
- Don't hold on to the past or expectations.
- Never give up.
- Unconditional love is the love Jesus has for us. He is our role model to emulate and follow when we try to express this type of love to others.
- The only way we can display unconditional love to others is falling back on what God has taught us about this love He designed.

Chapter 14: Grace

When talking about grace we need to recognize there are two ways to think about it. The first is God's grace for us. The second is our grace toward others. They are the same, but different all at the same time.

I watched a video recently about someone trying to explain grace. He was throwing piles of wet sand onto the beach and waves kept coming and washing it away. He was using the metaphor that his piles of sand were the mess we make and the waves were God's grace, and no matter what he did the waves kept coming to wash them away. It was a pretty interesting way of thinking about it. It doesn't matter what the circumstance, He will always pour out his grace onto us. What does the Bible say about grace?

> For it is by grace you have been saved, through faith—and this is not from yourselves, it is the gift of God—not by works, so that no one can boast (Ephesians 2:8-9).

> My grace is sufficient for you, for my power is made perfect in weakness (2 Corinthians 12:9).

Definition of *grace*:

The freely-given, unmerited favor and love of God.[9]

How hard is that? When someone wrongs us, we are to love them. When they hurt our feelings, we are supposed to forgive. That really goes against our human nature. It is such an intentional and deliberate action.

---

9. Dictionary.com Unabridged, s.v. "grace," Random House, Inc., http://www.dictionary.com/browse/grace (accessed: June 7, 2017).

The Other Side of the Struggle

It is not something that comes naturally to us; unfortunately, sin is what comes naturally to us. Lisa Chan in her video resource on the book *You and Me Forever*[10] talks about how her grandmother baked a cake for her alcoholic grandfather on his birthday. He was treating her poorly, like she was irrelevant and unimportant. She talks about the grace that she displayed to him even though he did not deserve it. What I really loved was what she said about how the world views that. The world tells us to leave, to dishonor, to walk away, to give up, and to not put up with any type of negative behavior. But the reality is that life is not perfect and it comes with baggage and hurt and broken people. The world may tell us to give up, but God tells us to forgive, to support, and to walk through the storms with people. It's a really hard concept for us to understand because our culture is drilling the opposite into our minds.

Can you think of people in your life or situations in your life where grace would be what you are called to give but not your first instinctual response? I can think of many. God gives us opportunities all the time to display His grace, but it's up to us to take advantage of them. Unfortunately, a lot of time we pass them up or don't even see them because we react before we think. Honestly, grace is probably the most difficult thing to give in a relationship, but something we almost expect when it comes to ourselves. It is so hard to forgive especially when it is not "deserved," yet when we do something wrong we beg and defend our way into getting people to extend grace to us. It's something our human brains really don't understand; it doesn't make sense that we should forgive someone or allow someone to "get away" with something if it's not warranted. The world teaches us that if someone wrongs us, we should do wrong to them back or hold it against them. Think about the times you have given someone the silent treatment when you are upset by something they did (if you're married this may be easier to picture). It's our nature to do this. It's ingrained in us to hurt people who hurt us and to treat people poorly when they treat us poorly. That is why it is such a backward concept for us to do the opposite, yet that's exactly what God does to us and what He asks us to do for others.

10. Lisa Chan, *You and Me Forever* (Claire Love Publishing: San Francisco, California), 2014.

So when it comes to the people in our life, especially the ones struggling, we need to offer grace toward them. So what are some practical ways we can challenge ourselves to display grace to others? Here's a couple of ways that I challenge you to try when everything in your being is trying to pull you the other way.

- Do not condemn.
- Empathize.
- Build others up.
- Forgive.
- Do not hold debt.
- Hold your tongue when you really want to add something to a situation that won't be productive, helpful, or supportive.
- Extend favor to someone who doesn't deserve your help.

Like I said, I challenge you to try these things and see what happens. You may be very surprised about what can happen as you walk in obedience to God's grace. Grace is the true meaning of what it means to deny ourselves, take up the cross, and give our lives up for Jesus. To be like Him means we need to be displaying grace more than anything.

Take Away

Things to Take Away from This Chapter:

- Two types of grace:
    1. God's grace toward us.
    2. Our grace toward others.
- Grace is not earned but given.
- Grace requires us to go against our natural instincts. The world teaches us that if someone wrongs us, we should do wrong back or hold it against them.
- Grace goes toward people who undeserving of it.
- Grace is probably the most difficult thing to give in a relationship but something we almost expect when it comes to ourselves.

Chapter 15: Speak Their Language

G ary Chapman opened to my eyes to something that changed my life forever—love languages.[11] We all have them and they determine how we both give and receive love. It's crucial to know what your spouse's love language is. In this difficult time, the best thing you can do is keep your spouse's love tank full. I know that this is a hard one to hear because they are likely not too "deserving" of this. For my husband, acts of service are his main love language.

Let me tell you a little bit about me—dishes are my nemesis. I actually have the strongest dislike for them in the world. When we were in the thick of darkness during one of our biggest battles to date, I felt God nudging me to do the dishes. I was appalled that He would even ask this of me—didn't He see that I was already doing everything else? I was taking care of the kids, the house, working full time, feeding everyone, and the list goes on and on! I felt like the one area my husband should be able to help me with was the kitchen. I resisted for a little bit in my stubbornness and being headstrong, but eventually God revealed to me why He was asking this of me. Even though it was not being shown (even worse, the opposite was being shown), my husband was hurting and feeling unlovable. Me doing the dishes had nothing to do with equality of work around the house but God asking me to do something specific and personal for my husband to show him he was loved in his own language. I started doing my best to keep the kitchen and dishes done. Looking back, that is one of the only tangible things my husband

---

11. Gary Chapman, The Five Love Languages, (Moody Publishers: Chicago, IL, 2009).

remembers that I did in those months. Had I decided to put my foot down and demand equal workloads in the house, I would have missed this opportunity to love my husband in the middle of his brokenness.

It really is the little things—the God orchestrated things—that make the difference; and trust me, you need those small differences to give you little glimmers of hope in the midst of the battle. Filling their love tank isn't going to change things drastically, but it's going to stand out. They will look back and see that when you could have been shutting them out and giving up, you were serving them in the language that they needed. My goal in doing this was to be an extension of God's love to him. This is how God loves us—even though we are not deserving of His love, He still gives it freely and unconditionally. This one is a hard pill to swallow, I get that, but I still encourage you to give it a try. How could it hurt, right?

The other part about speaking their language is understanding who they are as a person—what they need, what fills them up, what motivates them, and what overwhelms them. This comes down to our personality type, and more often than not we are dealing with people who are the complete opposite personality to our own. My husband and I could not be more opposite in our personalities; it is a blessing and a curse depending on the situation. There are so many positives to it—we balance each other out, we can see a situation from completely different viewpoints, and we bring out things in one another that are not naturally there. But there is another side to it, and if you don't know the other one well enough it can turn into quite a negative and offensive thing to the relationship.

We have done about eight personality, motivation, and even financial personality tests over the years, and I can say with one hundred percent certainty that taking those tests is why we are still married today. I will explain our situation in more detail to help you understand. There are so many different tests out there these days—ones that give you personality descriptions, ones that show what motivates you, ones that show you how you work best, even ones about how you spend money; the list is really endless. With each and every test we have ever taken, our results always end up on opposite sides of the spectrum. We haven't even had the same secondary personality on any test we have taken; we are polar opposites. I always half-joke that I have no idea how we ever started dating. I am the free spirit—fun-loving, optimistic, impulsive, everything-rolls-off-my-back type of personality. I don't put much thought into what I do or say before I do it (and that sometimes gets me in trouble). My husband is analytical, precise, a thinker, a perfectionist, and has a sometimes pessimistic (or a realistic, as he likes to call it) type of personality. He cannot just shoot from the hip or making quick decisions, he won't do something if he can't do it to the best of his ability.

Early on in our relationship, these personalities bumped heads a lot. They are so contradictory and different that had we not learned more about each other it would have ripped us apart. Once we learned about who each of us are, it explained so much and helped us understand why the other one does things that we would never think to do. For example, I used to get so offended when my husband would walk away during an argument, which would add more fuel into the fire of the argument from my point of view. My personality wants to deal with it immediately and move on. His personality needs to process; he needs time and space. My offense turned into understanding when I learned that he needed to walk away; he wasn't doing it to hurt me, and in all honesty it had nothing to do with me. He could not come to a point of resolve in the time frame that I was pushing on him. Learning to allow him to walk away also gave me the time I needed to cool down—time I would have never given myself because my personality is too quick and impulsive, trying to get things done as fast as I can. This is just one example, but one that I like to use to explain how our personalities need different things under different conditions. If you don't know that about your spouse, you are probably having many unnecessary arguments and hardships that could possibly be a result of your personalities combating each other.

Take Away

Things to Take Away from This Chapter:

- We all have different love languages; learn your spouse's and your own.
- Start to understand their personality—who they are and what they need.

Chapter 16: Set Your Expectations Realistically

Expectations are one of the biggest catalysts for conflict in marriage. There are different types of expectations I want to look at. First are the expectations we put on our spouse when they are in the middle of a struggle, second are the expectations we have of other people in our lives as we walk this difficult road, and third are expectations in our day-to-day life as a married couple.

I know when I give my husband expectations that are just not realistic for who he can be, ultimately I am the one who walks away disappointed and let down. If a person is in the midst of a battle of darkness, you have to be realistic of what you can expect from them. There have been times in my marriage when I literally had to take away any expectation and take it upon myself. If you know that putting more on their plate in this season of their life is causing more strife, you need to be willing to accept some of that responsibility and do something about it, because continuing with that demand will only end up negatively for everyone involved. Don't put things on them they can't actually handle. It just creates more problems. Yes, we want them to be a partner who can give in every area, but if that is just not feasible at that moment in time, acknowledge this and change things for the time being.

Your expectations of other people around you is another area to be aware of. When I try to explain why my husband struggles to other people, they (with good intentions) try to explain it back to me in very logistical and rational terms. This is one of the biggest things I have learned when dealing with mental illness: It is the opposite of logistical and rational!

The Other Side of the Struggle

It is not a linear path from point A to point B that can be dealt with the same as someone who doesn't struggle deals with something stressful or upsetting. It is like a zig-zag, up-and-down, back-and-forth loop-de-loop that makes absolutely no sense. When trying to communicate with my husband, if he is in a bad headspace I have to continuously remind myself of this because I will constantly try to bring rational thinking into it.

Let me give you an example. When we first moved across the country and things were starting to go downhill at a rapid pace, my husband was working at my parents' workplace and he was having the beginning of a long spiral. He ended up walking off the job and was sitting outside texting me, telling me that he was done with that job. My mom was very rationally asking why he couldn't just go back in and finish the shift and they would deal with it after. I knew that we were past the point of this happening, but I could understand her logical solution from her point of view. There was no way in that headspace he would get himself to the point of walking back in there, and I knew that. I truly could not explain this thought process to her in a way that made sense to a logical mind-frame.

This was a pivotal moment when I realized that when someone does not struggle, they bring rational thought into the situation. It isn't our fault or a bad thing; it is just a key point that shows you that if you do not struggle with mental illness, then as much as you try to understand and learn you cannot ever understand what it is like to be in the mind of someone who struggles with irrational and illogical thoughts. Our expectation is that they should be able to work within our rational mind-frame limits. But we actually set them up for failure when we put them in that place. Our expectations need to change so we can come into situations anticipating a realistic result from someone who is in a bad headspace.

The other part of expectations are the ones we make on our own. It comes down to the communication that is needed. I am sure you have heard this before, but once again I am here to remind you to communicate, communicate, communicate! If I decided during the day that we were going to have a family dinner and then spend time cuddling on the couch all night and he decided that he was going to finish building our pantry when he got home from work but neither of us communicated our plans with each other, when he got home and started working I would be upset because my expectations were not met. But how could they be met when we never communicated them? Now I sometimes will go as far as to ask, "These are my expectations of the night, what are yours?" It's amazing how many arguments are avoided this way. Another area of expectations is day-to-day functioning. Someone struggling does not react well to change, especially quick change. This is where communication is the only hope to defuse a spiral bomb. When we have plans and I go ahead and change them last minute, it usually ends up with some degree of a spiral.

There is another type of expectation that is harder to figure out—unwritten expectations. Everyone comes into a relationship and then marriage with unwritten rules they have and likely don't even know they carry. These are little things that can amount to bigger issues when not communicated. Things like where you put items in the fridge, or how you load the dishwasher, to bigger things like not putting your friends above your family or how you parent your children.

When my husband and I first lived together, it drove him up the wall where I took my shoes off and left them when I came home. I had no idea this bothered him or that he felt like shoes belonged in a certain area. One day, out of nowhere to me, he flipped out about the shoes. I was dumfounded because I had no idea this was an issue in the first place, so I could not figure out how it had already escalated to such a heated place. What he did not realize was that I didn't know that this was bothering him because he thought this would bother anyone. As we come into a relationship with two different upbringings, they have molded us into who we are. Now in marriage we have to adapt into a new life together. The smaller issues might be minimal and even funny, but even small things build up over time and can turn into enormous problems. We found it useful to sit down and think about what our "unwritten expectations" were. We wrote them down and stuck them on our fridge. It may seem silly, but this has been one of the most useful activities we have ever done.

The best solution to expectations is simply this—communication. If you can communicate together about your own expectations, you can avoid many arguments. If you can be aware of where your spouse's headspace is and know what they can handle at that time, you will be steps ahead of where the enemy wants you to be. Expectations can burn you or help you; it is about keeping them realistic and practical to determine their success.

Things to Take Away from This Chapter:

- Expectations are where the majority of disappointment stems from.

- Our expectations can either set others up for failure or success, and we need to understand that we have a role in which way that goes.

- Rational and logical thought processes are generally not part of the spiral. They may know the truth deep down, but their feelings and emotions are so out of whack that they have no place in that moment.

- There are expectations we put on our spouse when they are in the middle of a struggle.

- There are expectations we have of other people in our lives as we walk this difficult road.

- There are expectations that are in our day-to-day life as a married couple.

- Unwritten expectations—everyone comes into a relationship and then marriage with unwritten rules they have and likely don't even know they have.

- The best solution to expectations is simple—communicate.

Chapter 17: War for Your Spouse

I f you feel as though you are in the middle of a battle, you are. If you feel you are being hit by weapons like a target, you are. But what happens when your partner in life is being hit and can't defend themselves? It's a surreal experience to watch someone else being attacked by the enemy, especially when they can't see it or have been hit and cannot find the strength to get back up. We have been there; we are constantly the target of Satan's attacks. He knows our vulnerabilities, he knows our weaknesses, and he uses them against us at every opportunity he gets. When we got to our lowest of lows, I truly felt like I could see the battle for what it was. The spiritual war that is going on exists and is real. It is very easy to brush off because we cannot see it. When I had the opportunity to see and feel how real it was, that was when I went to war for my husband and our family.

I needed to start fighting back on behalf of my husband. I got to the point where I was so tired of seeing Satan try to take down my husband that I got mad; I was not going to stand for it anymore. I was in the middle of reading the book *Power of a Praying Wife* by one of my favorite authors, Stormie Omartian,[12] when I read something that completely changed my viewpoint, it spoke right into my mind and heart. We were on the day "Praying for His Mind" and it finally clicked in my head that Satan was attacking my husband, and my husband was a wounded soldier who could not fight back. We were married, so it struck me— why was I just sitting by and watching it happen? I needed to stand up

---

12. Stormie Omartarian, *Power of a Praying Wife* (Harvest House Publishers: Eugene, Oregon), 2014.

against the enemy; I needed to fight back with the strength that God was giving me. This hit me hard, like a punch in the stomach. What was I allowing to happen? Was I just complaining and asking God to "fix" it all these years while I moped around doing nothing? That was all I needed to take action. It was the fire under me that I needed. And that day I went to war.

If you are in a spiritual war, it is crucial to have constant communication in our relationship with God. For me, this wasn't my usual "fix him, but I'm all good" type of prayers. This was something entirely different. This was life-dependent prayer. This was "prayer-is-the-only-option" type of praying. I was saying to God, "Only You can change this situation." When I realized how serious and real the battle was, I felt like drastic measures were the only avenue to take. I literally got out a gallon of paint sitting in the back of a closet, took my three-year-old downstairs, and we emptied a freezing cold, gross, and messy closet and started painting. She asked, "Why are we painting?" I replied, "This is where we are going to pray for daddy," and we painted.

Then I got to work. I started praying down there, starting writing out Scriptures, prayers, and everything in between. I started praying for protection, for specific things that needed to be addressed. I started reading about how to pray for your spouse, which was so educational to the process. I then took it a step further and enlisted "prayer warriors." These were close, godly women whom I look up to, lean on, and who know the intricate details of the battle at hand. Some days I would just send them a text with a prayer request and sometimes it was an email with details and updates. Other times, it was down on our knees together praying united. Regardless of how you do this, you need people praying with you against the enemy's plans. The enemy has been at this game far longer than we've been around, he has tactics we don't know about, and it's important to have a support base while you are at war.

It doesn't matter what the circumstances are in your marriage—whether you are just growing apart, whether your husband is being tossed around by Satan, whether its financial burdens creating division, whether there's temptation trying to come between you; it doesn't matter. Your efforts alone will fall short. I know that it is hard to hear, but your energy needs to be focused elsewhere right now, so if the hard truth can save you wasting your time trying to control and fight this out alone, then I'm happy I said it. Take this situation and humbly bring it to God. Ask Him to reveal things to you that you need to hear. Ask Him to tell you when to go and when to stay. I have had moments when I was trying to intervene and God had to tell me to stop. It is so hard; it feels like you are giving up, but you are not. You are bringing it to the only Doctor who can fix it, and then you need to step out of the way and let God work.

In the midst of the darkest part of a recent battlefield we were in, God whispered to my heart, *Okay, Danielle, look at this situation. This is the results you get when you try on your own. Now let Me show you what I can do.* I can't explain in words what followed, but it can only be described as a miracle. God took a dead situation and resuscitated it back to life.

God is good; He wants good for us. When it comes to waring for your spouse it's not even about us, it's about taking it to God, who is already victorious against the enemy, and allowing Him to change the circumstances like only He can. Understand that you have the Creator of the Universe, the Almighty One, the Victor in any battle, and He is fighting for you and your marriage. How could that not encourage us? I challenge you, if you are in any season of your life where you feel like you should be fighting against the enemy for the sake of your spouse and your marriage, don't sit back and think it's all up to them—take a stand and fight the good fight!

Take Away

Things to Take Away from This Chapter:

- We need to fight back for our spouse.
- We need to lay it down at the cross, renege control, and allow God to take over.
- God will likely find areas for us to change as we come to Him.
- Let go and let God.
- It is crucial to have constant communication in our relationship with God.
- Enlist "prayer warriors."

Chapter 18: You Will Not Change Them by Your Own Strength

No amount of willpower or strength of mind will change a person. Only God can change a heart, a behavior, or a situation. God is going to be the One to get the person on board, and like we have looked at already, it will probably not be you.

What I have discovered to be victorious is to find success in the constraints of the given situation. Yes, sometimes it doesn't feel great, but what I have learned to do is to understand what we are dealing with and working within those boundaries for success. I have made a safe parameter for us that allows our marriage to thrive despite something that could tear it apart. I have changed my mentality to work with our obstacles rather than sulk about it not being "normal." If I allowed myself to set my expectations compared to someone's marriage who was not battling our obstacles then yes, it would be unfair, frustrating, and unequal. But as I personalize our situation, taking into account the obstacles we face, it allows the love to be seen. It allows me to feel supported, cared for, and loved by my husband, who may not always be in the best headspace to show those things to me by the world's standards.

I have come across several friends over the past months who are the "spouse/supporter" of someone who is struggling. It has been really interesting sharing our struggles. It is something only people dealing with that situation can understand, and it is very hard to talk with people who have never dealt with it before because they look at it from a very logical standpoint, which never works when you are dealing with a very illogical and unpredictable situation. It has also shown me that there is a missing link in the system because there is not a lot of support for the "other person" in the equation—the person who is on the other side of the struggle. Whether the person struggling is a spouse, girlfriend/boyfriend, family member, or close friend, we are just winging it half the time, going off of advice from people who don't know the whole story as we try to be the voice of reason in a confusing situation. It is definitely something to highlight that there are people affected other than the person who is struggling themselves.

I am writing this to highlight that not all the expectations of marriage or of relationships are what they seem. Sometimes you get handed a circumstance you never expected you would have to deal with in your lifetime, but I encourage you to find the beauty in it, because it is there. Under the mess, there is a blessing, and trust me when I say that God made no mistake when He put you two together. Find that reason, because it is always more encouraging and empowering than you could have ever imagined!

If you are in a position of supporting someone struggling, I want to encourage you to reach out and talk to someone—anyone you're comfortable with—and bring it to the light. That is of utmost importance—don't keep it in the dark. That is where Satan gains footholds, where you suffer alone. Don't ever believe the lie that you are better off keeping it to yourself. We are designed to walk this life with others, and sometimes that means reaching out when you need a shoulder to lean on when life gets heavy.

In the supportive role, we have mini-jobs that fall under this umbrella. Being a safe place for the struggler but not allowing abusive behaviors or getting taken advantage of is a fine line to walk. This is one of the hardest things to do because sometimes you just want to scream and shake them into snapping out of it. But that is that exact thing they struggle to do. This one takes patience and practice, both things I would say we all lack at times, but trust me when I say God's grace is the answer to this. If time and time again they see you being their safe place, they will eventually learn to trust that. And by you doing that, you become an example of what that looks like and can show them how it looks, and when they are in a better place they will be able to be that person for you. Love is not always butterflies and sunshine; sometimes it is walking a scary and dark road with someone and not giving up on them when it gets hard.

Sometimes your spouse can't be there for you when you are struggling with something yourself, which is likely going to be the case you encounter. It is important to surround yourself and set up safe places and support groups for yourself. I had some amazing people who held me through some dark times and allowed me to process and deal with my own issues when my husband couldn't. God was so good in that way, and now my husband can that person again, so, like I said, God is so good and each moment or season will end and give you a moment to breathe.

Life and relationships all come with unexpected curveballs, and if you find yourself in a position where you are dealing with something that may not seem "normal" to the world's standards of what that relationship should look like, it's okay. Don't compare, don't assume others have it all together (because the usually don't), and don't ever believe the lie that you cannot handle it, because we serve a powerful God who can handle anything, and He will give you the strength if you open your heart to Him.

Our biggest goal is supporting the struggler and guiding them to a place where they can get the help they need and, ultimately, the change that needs to take place. I believe we have great doctors, mental health counselors, and resources here on earth, but I know that without God all of that will fall short. I believe that guiding them back into a relationship with the Lord is the first and more important step. There will likely be many steps after that, and I am absolutely not against getting help from earthly resources. We were extremely lucky to get into an assessment program that dealt with diagnosis, support, resources, and medication that were all covered by our insurance. That will not always be the case, but more and more I am seeing communities that are starting to understand the need to help those struggling mentally and emotionally to be equally important as physical issues.

I know there is a rather controversial debate amongst Christians if using medication should be supported or not. My husband was adamantly against taking medication from the day I met him. It was not even on the table for discussion, and when I would encourage him to talk to someone he refused because he was convinced that they would just try and give him medication and he would be on his way. As you saw in our story earlier, it took things getting very ugly and dark for him to even consider going to talk to someone about getting help, and after that there were another three months before he would even try using medication. Sometimes medication is needed because there is a chemical imbalance. If you knew someone was diabetic and they told you they were refusing to take their medication, you would think they were nuts! It makes perfect sense to use medication when we talk about our physical problems, but when it comes to the mental side of it, all of a sudden there is controversy.

Sometimes medication can help with an extremely tough season that a person can't get out of. There are cases where medication is necessary every day, but God can work in that. My point in saying these things is that I watched someone suffer for six years, he himself struggled for twenty-two years, and after only weeks of trying medication every single person in his life was stunned by the good changes they saw in him, the amount mental clarity he had with just that little bit of help. If you are dealing with someone who will not take medication, don't give up, but also don't give them an ultimatum that they "have to or else." Backing people who struggle up against a wall is one of the worst things you can do. Although it took time and a lot of painful situations, a day finally came where my husband realized that he needed help outside of himself, and that was only after I gave it to God myself and went to war with Satan.

Take Away

Things to Take Away from This Chapter:

- Our will and desire for them to change will not be enough to actually change them.
- God is the only one with the power to change them.
- We can be a light and a safe place for someone struggling.
- Have your own support system that can hold you up when you are feeling weak and who will constantly bring you back to God.
- Bring it to the light and take away Satan's power in it from the darkness.
- Find the strengths within the limitations of the situation.
- Be a safe place for them, with boundaries protecting you.

Chapter 19: Go to God to Get Your Needs Met and Tank Filled

The big picture is this: We need to go to God to get *our* tanks filled and *not* to our spouse. This is the only source of lasting strength you will find. God needs to be the one filling our love tank, our energy tank, and every tank we have. Not only did He design it that way, it is the only sustainable way. No human being here on earth can fill us up high enough or long enough compared to what Jesus can do.

First of all, this isn't something you should be relying on your spouse to do in the first place. It comes down to keeping our expectations realistic and going to God for our needs. Our spouse cannot be where we go to be filled, regardless if they are struggling or not, but sometimes we fall into that trap even if we know that to be the truth. Second, Satan will offer you many fake and counterfeit ways to fill you up. He will design personal replicas of ways that you can feel fulfilled, but it is a scam and we must be aware of this because it will lead us to dangerous places.

The only way to do this is to spend time with God and immerse ourselves in His Word. It is a backward concept in our world in this day and age, but resting in God's Word is actually what re-energizes us. It is probably the most important thing to do in a time of catastrophe—prioritize this as just as important as eating and drinking.

If you take a serious and real look at your life, you will see areas where you are subconsciously expecting your spouse to fill you up. It might be when we are in a bad mood and expecting our spouse to change the entire situation because we want them to. We want them to say the right things, and if they don't the rest of the day is ruined. Our days, our moods, our behaviors, and most importantly our happiness should not be determined by what our spouse does. They are our partner on this journey of life, not the puppet master deciding how we feel and behave, so we can't see it as their fault when things aren't going smoothly.

You cannot keep going without getting your tank filled. You will burn out; you will fall and be discouraged and feel like you are failing. When we try to do it on our own, we don't get very far. God is the only source of unconditional outpouring of strength. It's very easy to get caught up in what the world can "offer" you. It's easy to be tricked by Satan to believe that something else can sustain you. Even things like sleep can feel like they help for a moment, but your emotional and mental capabilities will still be on overdrive.

I once led a study that asked the teenage girls I was teaching to give up the best time of their day to pray and spend with God. It was funny because as I asked them to try this out, I was convicted that I was not doing it myself. Sacrificing the best time of your day to Him will help your intimacy with Him. For me, this is the early morning when I am battling between ten more minutes of sleep in my warm bed or getting up. I'm telling you, when you sacrifice, He notices. God honors us when we do these things because they are the right things to do for our walk with Him. So get up early or give up whatever you need to so that you have some quiet and still time to read His Word and talk with Him. Pour out your heart, ask Him the questions, and write out your prayers. Do whatever you need to so that you are communicating with Him and pouring into your relationship with Him.

I can't count the number of times I have come to God and told Him that I could not continue in this supportive role and that I was done trying. I get weary, drained, and worn out from being beaten in the battle. Each of those times I have said to God, "If anything happens from here on out, it is all You, because I am throwing my hands in the air and giving up." God delivered me each and every time in those moments. He gave me an undeniable renewed strength, the right words to use, the right stance to take, and the right behavior to defuse the situation. His track record of coming into the situation when I have given up is one hundred percent, and I can say with great conviction that He always conquers whatever I issue bring to Him whenever I come to Him for help.

It really doesn't make sense to go to our spouses for a lasting supply of strength; they are mere humans just like we are. We have a God who tells us to come to Him, who has the power to provide this for us.

> Come to me, all you who are weary and burdened, and I will give you rest (Matthew 11:28).

> But those who hope in the Lord will renew their strength. They will soar on wings like eagles; they will run and not grow weary, they will walk and not be faint (Isaiah 40:31).

> Be strong and take heart, all you who hope in the Lord (Psalms 31:24).

So when we really look at it, we are setting our spouses and marriages up for failure when we ask for things that are out of their ability to give us. Next time you are becoming frustrated or discouraged with your spouse for something you are asking of them, remember this concept and see if you are asking them for something you should really be asking God for.

Take Away

Things to Take Away from This Chapter:

- Your spouse cannot fill up your tank; only God can.
- Do not put the responsibility on someone else to fill you up, especially someone who is struggling to stay afloat themselves.
- Give up the best time of your day and spend it with God.
- When you are empty, God will fill you up and give you an undeniable strength that is not from you but given to you by Him.

Chapter 20: Look Inward

I want to encourage you to "spy on yourself." I know that sounds weird, but hear me out. When my husband was going through his struggle, I ran into God's arms. I truly felt like I did everything right; I felt like my eyes were focused on God so deeply that I was a rock. Unfortunately, I wasn't, and Satan is an opportunist and jumped in on that very deceitfully.

I hurt my back and starting taking some medication to help with the pain. Within days, my life fell apart with my husband's mental illness going off the deep end. Without even realizing it, I became dependent on those pills. It finally clicked to me that it was becoming a problem once I realized I was taking them when I wasn't even in pain. By then it was too late; it had become an addiction and an escape from the emotional baggage my life encompassed at the time. After becoming aware of what was going on, the next issue I had to work through was the battle to bring it to the light and acknowledge the problem. I actually went weeks aware of the problem and knowing what I was doing was wrong, but Satan kept saying all the right things to keep me there. Finally, after a long time I confided in my husband and a really good friend (who happens to also be an addiction counsellor) who helped guide me to the right place so I was able to start the process of getting help and dealing with the issue in a healthy way.

After I started to deal with that, I realized that I had picked up another negative coping mechanism—I had started turning to food to cope. In a matter of months, I had gained a huge amount of weight, higher then I had ever been even after having two kids. What I had subconsciously done was dropped one bad habit for another. The biggest and scariest part of this was I was not even connecting these problems to the chaos and unpredictability of living with someone who was struggling. I was not seeing that when my husband had bad days, I was doing things to soothe myself in another area of my life. I was so convinced I was being strong and handling things so well that it took a very long time for me to finally connect the two. I also learned, as I looked back on my own life, that addiction was there. It was there in my teens and young adulthood with drugs and alcohol and then turned to eating and, honestly, probably even an addiction to love and to my relationships. What I learned through this experience with the pill addiction was that the root cause had never been dealt with, only the symptoms; that is why when I would drop one addiction I would just pick up another.

I ended up connecting with an addiction counseling service in my hometown and started the process of working on my own issues. Why I am telling you this? So you can be aware that Satan will take advantage where you are weak, and as you are relying on God the enemy will get more and more personal until he can break you. I believe that knowing this gives you an advantage to prevent this tactic from working.

My second point is that anything can become negative; Satan can even take wonderful, godly things and make them idols. This is why my advice is to "spy on yourself." Make sure you know why you are doing everything you are doing and that you are holding your thoughts, actions, and behaviors in captivity to God's standard. Why? Because as you battle in the war you are going directly up against the enemy, and as you are standing firm with God, the harder the enemy fights. I urge you to not go based on the feeling that you are doing okay, because when there is something serious going on in your life it is our human nature to deflect it to something else, whether we realize it or not. As much as you may think you are being strong, something may be falling out the bottom that you are not even seeing. This is why self-awareness and continuously looking inward is so important in case you are doing something to alleviate or self-medicate from the stress and heavy load you are carrying.

I have recently been learning how to garden. It is quite a steep learning curve for this city girl, and I have made quite a lot of mistakes. With certain plants like tomatoes, they have "runners," which are little stems that grow but will never produce fruit. If they are not tended, all the plant's energy will go into these fruitless runners and there will not be enough energy to grow the actual fruit. How metaphorical. How many "runner" behaviors and idols do we have in our lives? How much energy are we putting into fruitless things, things that are taking away from what God has planned for us?

The Bible says in John 15:5, "I am the vine; you are the branches. If you remain in me and I in you, you will bear much fruit; apart from me you can do nothing."

So if Christ is the vine and we are the branches, then we can only produce fruit because of Christ. For that to happen, God must prune the runners that will not produce fruit. The tough part about pruning is that it hurts; it's sacrificial and it's hard for our selfish nature.

> But the fruit of the Spirit is love, joy, peace, forbearance, kindness, goodness, faithfulness, gentleness and self-control. Against such things there is no law (Galatians 5:22-23).

These are the fruits produced with direct connection to the vine. But we live in a fallen world that is filled with deception, sin, and distraction. If we are putting our energy in our "runner" stem, then we are getting the opposite of fruit.

Tim Keller has a great comparison of this.[13]

Fruit	Opposite
Love	Fear leading to self-protection resulting in the harm of others.
Joy	Despair and a lack of or fear of hope.
Peace	Worry and anxiety.

---

13. September 5, 2011. Date accessed: August 2016, http://www.jdgreear.com/my_weblog/2011/09/kellers-definitions-of-the-fruit-in-galatians-5.html.

Fruit	Opposite
Patience	Bitterness and resentment toward God that manifests itself in agitation or outright expressions of anger with others.
Kindness	The inability to rejoice in the good happening to others.
Goodness	Hypocrisy, phoniness, and insincerity.
Faithfulness	Opportunistic living that swings from committed to absent.
Gentleness	Thinking you are superior leading to self-absorption and self-promotion that crushes others.
Self-control	Impulsive living in the moment.

John 15:2 says, "He cuts off every branch in me that bears no fruit, while every branch that does bear fruit he prunes so that it will be even more fruitful." So if we are pouring our energies into the opposite of the fruit listed above, God says He will cut those off so they can bear no fruit. So how does He prune those branches? Pruning is a process that God uses for our best interests, to help us and for our good. Even though the pruning may hurt at times, we need to remember God is good and only does good and that pruning is just that—for our good.

When pruning something large, like a tree, there are a few different tools you may need. Sometimes you need something like a chainsaw to get large and rooted branches, and sometimes smaller tools can get smaller branches more delicately and not injure anything around them. Likewise, God has different tools He uses to prune us.

The Hand Pruner = God's Word

God's Word is the perfect tool for pruning. It is soft yet sharp and can take away those fruitless branches without harming you in the process. It uses truth and biblical experiences to help change your heart back to the vine and convicts your heart to make that change.

The Chainsaw = Trials

Sometimes our fruitless branches are deep-rooted and have had years to build up strength so it takes more than words to break them off. Trials are big circumstances that force us to deal with things that we are not dealing with and need to be. It is a forceful pruning process that requires us to be broken down, vulnerable, and picked at.

A very encouraging Scripture from *The Message*, reads, "No test or temptation that comes your way is beyond the course of what others have had to face. All you need to remember is that God will never let you down; he'll never let you be pushed past your limit; he'll always be there to help you come through it" (1 Corinthians 10:13). Pruning is a crucial aspect to the health of our walk. We will succumb to terrible things without it, just like a tree would if it did not have those branches taken away. It is unhealthy to keep them with us. It allows us to grow deeper in our relationship with Christ. It takes away the things we are doing or lies we are believing that stand in the way of our relationship with Him. These unfruitful characters act as a block—a divide that comes between us and our walk. By pruning them away, we are able have that direct connection again. So, as uncomfortable and difficult the pruning process is, try and welcome it and allow it to do what it's supposed to do. In the long run—the bigger picture—it is for your benefit, although that isn't always easy to see. Keep pressing on; lean on God and not your own understanding of the situation. As God prunes you, He is shaping you into who He created you to be. Allow this to happen; it is worth it!

Take Away

Things to Take Away from This Chapter:

- Spy on yourself.

- Satan is an opportunist.

- When your focus on so intensely on someone else, Satan will find ways to try and make you fall yourself.

- Self-awareness and continuously looking inward is so important to keep yourself in check.

- Allow God to prune you so you can have the closest and most intimate relationship with Him you can have.

Chapter 21: It Will Not Change Overnight

The reality of the situation is this: It will not change overnight. In fact, when dealing with something like mental illness, there are aspects of it that may never go away. It can be a very despairing place to be. We live in a culture of instantaneous results and quick fixes, so it has becoming increasingly hard for us to wait for God's perfect timing. God's plans for us involve many different lessons in them, and that takes time, especially when we are resisting the lesson in the first place. God allows suffering and hardships because they change us— they tear us down and put us in a position where He can work.

What you need to understand is the road to healing is a marathon, not a sprint. It takes training, discipline, removing things that are holding you down, overcoming obstacles, and allowing God to prune away the areas that cannot come with you on the other side. Because this road can take time, there will be moments and even seasons of discouragement along the way.

Sometimes that discouragement can be paralyzing. It's hard to make the next move or take the next step when you are feeling the weight of it all on your shoulders. It is a very tough place to be. I have been there. I have been in situations where I was taking leaps of faith and trying to walk according to what I believe God's will is for my life, and I was continuously running into obstacles that stopped me right in my tracks. It has been such a frustrating process trying to not let it take over my mind. It isn't easy and it feels incredibly "all-consuming" and it is hard to fight. The worst part is knowing that this is part of the enemy's game; he wants this, wants me to give up, to believe the lies that I am not good enough so I will quit and not continue on working within God's plan. As I walk this road, I am going to come into those moments of discouragement I just described. I have had to face it before and I will surely have to face it again. In my heart I know where I need to go—I need to run into Jesus's arms and let Him work in this. If you are walking in discouragement in an area of your life, let's walk through it together.

What should we do? Like I said before, run to Jesus. How does that look? Open your Bible, put some worship music on, get on your knees, and open your heart and mind to Him. Once, I sat down with my Bible and opened it to an area of various topics and found "discouragement" and read all the verses I could find about it. It is very helpful to be immersed in God's light to battle against Satan and his tactics.

It is important to stand guard against what the enemy will have up his sleeve. He sees you vulnerable and discouraged and he will use the opportunity to see if you will bite at what he is offering. It is easy to find negative coping mechanisms in this world. When you're feeling low, these seem like they can be very helpful. It can be anything from eating terrible food to turning to alcohol/drugs to hurting yourself. You need to be aware. Satan likes to present these negative coping skills with a positive twist that imitates a good thing. He will use your personal weaknesses to find ways to get into your mind. Stand guard against his ways. When you are feeling upset he will feed you lies—most often lies that are attached to some part of a truth to try to trick you into believing them. The opposite and more offensive side to this is to find yourself some healthy coping skills to combat the moments you feel discouraged.

For me, it's writing. When I get overwhelmed and dispirited I tend to let it fester, let Satan get more and more lies into my head. I have learned that once I sit down at my computer and start writing, it is amazing how different I feel, how much stronger I feel to fight, how much those lies seem pathetic. Find your healthy outlet. It can be anything as long as it's not taking you further away from God. Exercise, reading, talking to someone, sports, cooking, the list can go on forever. Whatever it is, take it seriously. If you are finding yourself in a discouraging place, be intentional about doing something about it. The longer it sits in the dark, the more of a hold Satan gets on it.

Another thing to do is ask God, "What am I supposed to learn?" Nothing is wasted with God. He always has a plan and He will use every part of your journey—the good, the bad, and even the ugly. So the first thing you can try to do is ask yourself, "What is the lesson here? What is God trying to teach me?" In my case, relying on Him for strength and following His footsteps instead of creating my own are a part of my lesson. The quicker you figure out the lesson, the quicker you can be out of the feeling of discouragement and being upset. It's very easy to focus on the negative. I had a conversation recently that I could probably very easily tell you every negative point I took from it and would struggle to remember the positive. It can be helpful to take a piece of paper and write down the positive points. It can surprise you how easily you overlooked them once they are on the paper in front of you!

Never forget to look at God's truth.

> The righteous cry out, and the Lord hears them; he delivers them from all their troubles. The Lord is close to the brokenhearted and saves those who are crushed in spirit. The righteous person may have many troubles, but the Lord delivers him from them all (Psalms 34:17-19).

> He heals the brokenhearted and binds up their wounds (Psalms 147:3).

> Cast your cares on the Lord, and he will sustain you; he will never let the righteous be shaken (Psalms 55:22).

> So do not fear, for I am with you; do not be dismayed, for I am your God. I will strengthen you and help you; I will uphold you with my righteous right hand (Isaiah 41:10).

> But those who hope in the Lord will renew their strength. They will soar on wings like eagles; they will run and not grow weary, they will walk and not be faint (Isaiah 40:31).

The Other Side of the Struggle

We will face discouragement along the way; it is unfortunately inevitable. But if you allow God to work through it, it will not destroy you but make you stronger. Life is just unfair sometimes; it's just the truth. People will let you down, this world will let you down, but Jesus will never let you down. So I encourage you today to do something positive to help yourself in your discouraging moment—to run into Jesus and let Him show you what He can do with it.

Take Away

Things to Take Away from This Chapter:

- This is a journey and it takes time to walk it.
- It is a marathon, not a sprint; you may not see changes for a long time.
- You cannot change anyone else; the only you can control is yourself, your attitude, your commitment, your behavior.
- Discouragement and despair are common feelings on this journey.
- Like always, we need to run to Jesus.
- Always ask God, "What am I supposed to be learning? What is my lesson in this?"

Chapter 22: Hopelessness

I want to walk you through some misconceptions and misunderstandings of what it is it like to be living in the darkness. Something I have seen over and over again when either talking to or learning about someone who is struggling is that the state of hopelessness consumes them and is incredibly hard to get out of. I have tried over the years to do some research about this and only found very run-of-the-mill answers. I want you to see into the mind of someone struggling, so I have combined my own experiences and those of other people in my life along with credited research to try to do that.

An old friend from high school who was in my life throughout university took his own life. It was shocking news to hear. Although I hadn't seen him in years, it was not news I expected to hear. What was amazing was the outpouring of love and support from those in his life after it happened. It was incredible to see how loved he was and heartbreaking to know how sad everyone was as well. My husband and I started to talk about hopelessness and something he said stuck in my mind. He said, "When I was at my lowest point, in my darkest moments, it didn't matter how much people loved me—I couldn't see it or feel it."

I had walked this darkness with my husband and was his main supporter during that dark time and I can attest that this was true. Nothing I said or did during that time would truly have gotten him out of that darkness or made him understand the reality of the support and love he did have.

The scariest place to be in life is consumed by hopelessness—to not feel purpose, to be overtaken by darkness, to have no will to go on. That is exactly where the enemy wants you to be—to feel as though you could not be further from God. That feels victorious for the devil. What breaks my heart is how many people in this world are stuck in that exact place. What breaks my heart even more is the lack of understanding and education those who don't struggle have. It simply is not that easy to "snap out of it" or to "get over it." It just doesn't work like that. Let's take a walk through the mind of someone who is struggling and look into the obstacles that overtake the mind in their headspace.

What It's Really Like

Built on a Bed of Lies

Satan has usually been at work for a while by the time they start feeling hopeless. We all have lies we believe, but sometimes as someone gets bombarded with endless lies it become truth and reality to their heart and soul. These are lies of worthlessness, being unlovable, and feeling unqualified. They are told that they are uneducated, unable, and forgotten by God. These lies build up, and after hearing them over and over again, they become truth in someone's heart. These lies create a perfect petri dish for hopelessness to be born and start to grow.

Darkness

This is not just a tough moment or day; it is being consumed by darkness all the time—a darkness so consuming that it's not possible by your own strength to get out, no matter how much you want to. It is a defeated place, and not only do you not want to put in the effort to get out, you have absolutely no desire to either. It gets to the point where the darkness actually becomes comfortable and happiness and light become scary and uncomfortable.

Loss of Interest

For my husband, rock climbing is his passion. When he didn't even want to do this, I knew we were in deeper than I understood. It is not just feeling like you don't want to do something for a day, it is a complete loss of desire to do the things you truly love. And even when you do them, they don't give you the same fulfillment they once did, and that is even harder to grasp.

Can't See the Positive Side of Things

I am an optimistic person for the most part. After I had both my girls I struggled with postpartum depression, and this was very challenging. I lost the ability to see past my bad mood and see the positive side of things. Many people who have a mental illness struggle with this one even more. Their default frame of mind or viewpoint is negative. It takes such effort and commitment for them to not immediately go a pessimistic and cynical place.

More Than a Bad Mood

Its more than an hour; it's more than not getting your way; it's more than just plain old being in a bad mood. It's also more than being able to just snap out of it; it's more than getting over something. It literally has taken over your mind and body and you feel powerless to be stronger than it.

It's Uncontrollable and They Don't Want This Either

This is not how they want to live or act. They don't want to go through life hurting the ones closest to them, but they are. Like we have already looked at, they can't snap out of it so they can't stop it by their own will. Of course, this isn't an excuse to continuously hurt or abuse people, but just know that as they are hurting people, deep down they don't want or desire to do that. It's almost like a symptom of the real problem occurring.

Defense Mechanisms

When someone is struggling, they start to create defense mechanisms to protect themselves. For my husband, pushing me away or shutting me out was his way of protecting himself. Subconsciously, he had started believing that "if I hurt you, you cannot hurt me." The hardest part for both of us is that he did not mean or want that, he just did not have any other way to cope and would default to this process every time he got into a bad headspace.

It Hurts

I know it looks like it doesn't affect them at all, but deep down it does. Deep down there are hurts beyond our understanding—deep wounds that are not healed and are so painful. There is a common saying, "Hurt people, hurt people."

They Feel That You Are Better Off without Them

I don't just mean suicidal thoughts, but that is certainly a common mentality with people struggling. They often feel guilty that they are such a burden, that they cannot be the equal person you want them to be and they desire to be. They feel that if they were out of your life, your life would be better. This is a thought process that I have come across over and over again when talking to people who struggle. In their heart, they truly believe that your life would be better without them around.

They Are Silently Crying Out for Help

Without words, gestures, or even actions, they are so desperately trying to get out. They want to get out; no one wants to live in darkness even if they believe they do. I know that it looks the complete opposite in actions and behaviors. The defeat and darkness they are experiencing overtakes any possibility to show this truth. Don't go on for years and years like I did, making excuses for every time something happened until I finally realized they were all moments of unconsciously crying out for help.

Take Away

Things to Take Away from This Chapter:

What it is really like for the struggler?

- Built on a bed of lies.
- Darkness.
- Loss of interest.
- Can't see the positive side of things.
- Its more than a bad mood.
- It's uncontrollable and they don't want this either.
- Defense mechanisms.
- It hurts.
- They feel that you are better off without them.
- They are silently crying out for help.

Chapter 23: What You Can Do

One thing that helped me continue supporting and believing during the darkest of moments were these little glimmers of hope God gave me along the way. I once read a story about a family hiking with a toddler. Each time the toddler would get tired and whiney, one of the parents would run ahead and put a chocolate candy on a rock ahead, just far enough away, but yet close enough for them to see. The child would get a surge of energy and run toward that chocolate. This continued the entire way up the mountain. This story always resonates with me because God has always put out His own chocolate candies for me when I start to doubt or become exhausted by the whole ordeal. They have been anything from a surprise friend showing up to talk, to an epiphany or revelation I discover in my time with Him, to the best and most motivating one—a glimpse of who my husband really and truly is shining through, the person I fell in love with, the loving and kind person that he is underneath all the darkness. Those "candies" have kept me going time and time again. I urge you, keep your eyes open for these moments because God is so good in taking care of us along the way. He will always be placing these chocolate candies for us to get up the mountain, but we need to be looking for them too.

There is a lot we can do for the success of coming out on the other side stronger and with a resilient relationship. We have to remember that rationality and logic are not always going to be successful here, so we need to approach this in a different and creative way to show our support and walk through this difficult time with them. The most success is found on the preventative—preparing your own heart, thoughts, and behaviors. You cannot control anything they say or do, but you can control what you do and you can prepare your own heart, thoughts, and behaviors for when things start going into a darker place.

Have an Understanding Mind

Expecting them to snap out of it or be in a good mood because they ate or slept isn't realistic. It's not realistic to think this is a twenty-four-hour flu. It's much deeper than that, and unfortunately, if you are in their life, you need to change what you are asking of them because, in all reality, they can't handle much right now. You need to try and empathize and understand how they feel to be able to look past the symptomatic behavior that is coming out making things cloudy. This is where compassion and sympathy are tools that need to be used constantly.

Silence Sometimes Really Is Golden

One of the most successful things I have learned and am still trying to perfect is the concept of knowing when to keep my mouth shut and when it is appropriate to give my "two cents." This takes an incredible amount of self-discipline, and even though I try very hard, I slip up in this area the majority of the time. Once we get involved emotionally and give them reactions, it just adds fuel to the fire. We all say things in the heat of the moment, but when we strike back it almost always creates more division, more disconnect, and will take much longer for the spiral to be over. Learning and then perfecting the skill of being silent is something we can do to help some situations not progress into an argument and get ourselves involved when we don't need to be.

Find Ways to Support Them without Words

Words unfortunately go in one ear and out the other to someone struggling with deep issues. Try and find personal acts you can do that will stand out to show your support. We looked at filling them up in their own love language, which can be without words unless their love language is words of affirmation.

Listen

Going along with being silent is to listen, both to what they are saying and to what they are not saying. Many times people who are struggling are crying out for help without even using their words. Sometimes their words only express half of what they are feeling and they hide the other half. We need to be attentive to all these areas to find the foundation of how they are actually feeling, because that is the area we need to support. Sometimes when we are listening, we are actually trying to hear things *we want* to hear; that is not the goal here. We need to listen to what their heart is saying, and that is how we can find personal ways to encourage them.

Your Desire to Change Them Won't Work, So Stop Trying

I get this, trust me. I wanted my husband to get better so badly that I tried everything in my willpower. Notice my wording—*my* willpower. That just isn't enough. It wasn't until I seriously and wholeheartedly took our situation to God and gave up my own will that things started to change. It's important to say it like that because I took our situation to God in the wrong way and with the wrong heart many times for years and nothing was happening. It's important that you are humbly coming to God and laying it down at His feet.

Compartmentalize

This was the best advice I got from a councilor I was seeing. She told me to compartmentalize my husband's behavior in a bad headspace away from who he is as a person when he is not in a bad headspace. It was extremely helpful because he is not a bad person, and sometimes the choices he makes in a bad headspace make it seem otherwise. When I began to separate the two, it helped me see the loving husband and amazing father he is without adding the negative to that perspective.

God Will Likely Ask You to Change First

When I first took our situation to God, He started to change my heart and ask me to do things. (I remember distinctively asking Him if He heard me and saying, "I'm not the problem here, God!") But there are things you can be doing, things that God needs of you to heal the situation. Listen to Him and follow what He is asking because there is a reason for it. Allow Him to work; He is much wiser then we are and sees the bigger picture. From experience, I urge you to listen and obey what God is telling you.

Prepare Yourself for the Unpredictable

Having someone in your life with mental illness equals a very unpredictable life. You don't know what you are going to face each day—how they will react to what life throws at them. If they are in a good place, you aren't sure how long it will last. If they are in a bad space, you don't know when it will be over. This can create a lot of anxiety for you as the supporter. Trying to get to a place of flexibility is tough, but will help you in the long run. Sometimes things are going so well until something triggers a spiral, and you have to be prepared at a moment's notice to take over family life for the rest of that time. I have been the supporter for so long that I have adjusted to this, but in the beginning it was overwhelming and chaotic.

Awareness

Your situation is personal to you and your spouse. What works for me may not work for you. Becoming aware of how they act during a bad headspace, what they need, what is good for them, and what is not good for them can go a long way. If you know it helps to give them a little space and time alone, then set that up for them. If you know that trying to talk about things in the midst of a situation will only escalate things and make things go further into the vortex of darkness, then learn how to patiently wait until they are mentally ready to deal with it. The more and more you start to become aware of what works and what doesn't work for them, the better you can handle the bad headspaces when they come along.

Make an Action Plan with Your Spouse When You Are Both in a Good Headspace

When both of you are in a good headspace, sit down and write out an action plan. This involves them in the process and they can feel empowered and give some helpful solutions. Although your spouse may not enjoy you following through when they are in a bad headspace, they will at least have the knowledge of why you are doing what you are doing, and also there is a sense of participation and involvement on their part. It will take a consistent follow-through from your end to show them that you are taking it seriously, that you are enforcing the boundaries in the plan, and that this can be a predictable reaction they can expect from you each time they fall apart. Having them involved in the creation of the plan is key to the success and how they will receive it when you do try and implement it.

Try and Figure Out What They Need

Do they do better with space? Do they do better if you are there with them? It is important to know how to set them up for success because they are not strong enough to do it themselves. For my husband, he needs space and he usually needs something physical. As a climber, getting outside, even if it is just on the wall on our property, can be helpful. The problem is, once he is past a certain point in the spiral he just wants to isolate himself and ignore the world. It takes a lot of encouragement to get him to get outside to do something for himself. If I can catch it before he goes too deep into the spiral, I can convince him to get out and do something for himself. If you know what they need in advance, it can be helpful so you can remind them of something they can do as self-care that they would probably not initiate on their own.

Learn As Much As You Can Yourself

There are a lot of mental illness resources in the world right now right at your fingertips. This is not an area to be ignorant or uninformed because that will only hurt you and your spouse. There are many things to learn about what not to do, something we will explore next, but even that will just touch the surface. Learning all you can about the specific type of illness you are dealing with can help you in so many ways and help you find how to be more specifically supportive to your spouse.

The Other Side of the Struggle

Be an Unchanging Witness

I encourage you to not hide the fact that you are relying on God to your spouse, but I also encourage you not to push it down their throat. It is important to show them where your strength is coming from and to redirect their gaze back to God. It is more of a subtle and consistent witness that you can be to them without words, but by your actions. Are you reading your Bible on a daily basis? Are you praying for both sides of the situation, even when it is hard? Are you being supportive when the world would tell you to walk away? (Again, this excludes abuse.) Is your attitude positive and God-driven rather than engulfed by the negativity of the situation? Like the old saying goes, "Actions speak louder than words," and this is a case where that could not be more true. When someone is struggling, there is a high chance there is a spiritual aspect to it. When Satan has someone in the darkness, he wants them to stay there and will do anything to make that happen. This makes it harder to witness and bring Jesus into the situation when someone is already defensive and distrustful before you even come in. When my husband was in the thick of a spiral, bringing up God or prayer received a very unpleasant reaction almost all of the time. You have to remind yourself that you are fighting Satan and not your spouse. This is also why actions are much more well-received than your words. Also, by being consistent it shows them you are not just reading your Bible and praying just because you don't know what else to do (which may be how you feel, in all honesty) but that you trust God all the time, and that is where the witnessing really happens. All I know is that when my husband looks back to the darkest moments in our journey, I can only hope that what stands out was my reliance and dependency on God through it. No amount of understanding or support could have been sustained on my own, so my goal in the past and going forward is that I redirect all the glory and triumph back to the One who is really the basis of where it came from.

Take Away

Things to Take Away from This Chapter:

What you can do for the success of the situation:

- Have an understanding mind.
- Silence sometimes really is golden.
- Find ways to support them without words.
- Listen.
- Your will to change them won't work, so stop trying.
- Compartmentalize.
- God will likely ask you to change first.
- Prepare yourself for the unpredictable.
- Awareness.
- Make an action plan with your spouse when you are both in a good headspace.
- Try and figure out what they need.
- Learn as much as you can yourself.
- Be an unchanging witness.

Chapter 24: What Not To Do

There are many things we do that actually make things worse, and we don't even realize we are doing them. It is really important to look at the other side of things and make notes to ourselves about what we should not be doing. Unfortunately, there are many things that cause more stress and problems to the already stressful situation. Sadly, we are sinful beings who succumb to our feelings far too often, and they follow the enemy's plan to destroy. Engaging and becoming emotionally involved in a spiral situation can actually be doing more harm than good for the both of you. We all say things we don't mean when we get upset, and in the heat of an argument even two level-headed people can let the emotions flare up when in anger. This becomes greatly intensified and has more of a long-term effect when it comes to someone struggling. It's important to know where your personal guidelines are and where you are hurting the situation by what you are doing and saying. I learned a lot of these lessons the hard way, so if I can help at least one person not to make a hard situation harder, that is worth it to me.

Do Not Engage

One of the worst things I have found I can do when my husband is in a bad headspace is engage in it with him. When I engage, I am suddenly emotionally involved and then it is really easy to start focusing on surface-level problems, which can get turned around on me very quickly and easily. When anyone is hurting, they will want to shift the blame to someone else and the focus gets off of them. This makes it easy when you come into the situation and start participating in the spiral. When you engage, all of a sudden you are in this vortex with them and it is so incredibly hard to get out once you are in. You are far better off to lay

149

out your boundaries, remove yourself, and wait until they are in a clearer headspace to involve yourself. I have to continuously remind myself of this because once something gets said personally about me, I tend to jump in emotionally because I react impulsively; then all of a sudden I am involved and have to deal with the ramifications of that.

Tell Them to Snap Out of It

This is probably one of the worst things you can do. "Getting over it" or "snapping out of it" is not something they are capable of doing. By demanding this, it builds up more of a wall in between you and them. They will not feel supported by you when you are asking them to do something they may so desperately want to do but cannot. Trust me when I say this—if they could snap out of it, they would. This demoralizes them even more.

Compare to Other Situations, Especially Worse Ones

Telling them other people's situations is not helpful to someone who is struggling. Even if there are many people struggling with worse situations, that is not going to cause someone struggling with mental illness to not focus on themselves. It actually makes them feel worse because, logically, they know there are others worse off, so it makes them feel worse that they are even struggling.

Get Frustrated Because It Is All about Them

I am very guilty of this one. I used to always say, "Oh, here comes another pity party." I would get so fed up with it being all about him all the time. But it is not productive to reiterate to them that it not all about them and that they can't feel sorry for themselves. I am sure there is a much more psychological term for this, but in layman's terms this is what I mean. They are in a very weird headspace where they are so low, especially about themselves, but then also make it about themselves and dwell on how terrible it is for them.

Push Them Too Much and Too Hard

I used to be so determined to force my husband to come to church or small group, even if he was having a terrible spiral. What I have learned over the years is that I was partially trying to make him come so I feel better, so we look better and no one would think anything is wrong. Second, pushing him to do it ends up backfiring almost every time. I have learned that sometimes I have to go to an event alone because mentally he cannot be there. Even though we have overcome so much in our walk with mental illness, we still encounter days when I attend things alone.

Tell Them They Are Doing It for Attention

There might be some truth to that statement because when we are hurting we tend to lash out in ways that are trying to get some attention. The problem lies in trying to communicate that to them while they are in the midst of a bad headspace. Although it may be true, it is probably best not to throw that in their face in the heat of the moment.

Give In to Them If They Are Pushing for a Reaction

There have been times when my husband was in such chaos and darkness in the moment he was in that he would try and turn it around and bring me down with him. Misery loves company, right? It is very important to recognize that it is not about you, but if you engage with it, on the surface it will turn into it being about you in a negative way. Learn to walk away when things start to turn that way and it will save you a lot of your own emotional heartaches.

Compare Their Situation to Yourself

There is a chance that you have gone through tough times in your life, and even if you struggled with depression, addiction, or even mental illness in your past, *if you are not currently dealing with it, you will never convince them you know what they are going through.* Their frame of mind is that they are the only ones feeling this particular way and that no one could possibly understand how they feel. Trying to convince them any differently by comparing their situation with your own is probably not the best avenue. Now, it is very important to try and show them that they are not alone, that others struggle very similarly to them with positive outcomes, but if they are in the midst of a bad headspace, that is not the time to try and get that point across.

The Other Side of the Struggle

Label Them

Their illness does not define them in the same way someone battling a physical illness is not only seen as their disability. If they do have a diagnosis of which mental illness or depression you are dealing with, the last thing you want to do is call them by that name. Their struggle is only a part of who they are, and although it seems like it has taken over every aspect of who they are, it hasn't. We need to compartmentalize and separate who they are from their illness. On top of their diagnosis label, we also subconsciously label them things like weak, selfish, broken, and much more along those lines. Like I said, it may even be subconscious, but we need to be very careful. Our words and our role in this situation matter a lot to the struggler, even if they are not showing that.

Blame Their Relationship with God

This reminds me of Job's friends. Telling someone struggling that it is their fault or something they have done to cause this is not the approach to take. We need to do anything and everything we can to walk them closer to God; He is the only One who can truly bring any change and healing into the situation. Telling them that this is caused by their broken relationship with God is going to drive them further away from Him and make the chances of them coming back to Him lower and lower. There is a good chance if they are in the midst of the darkness their relationship with God is being affected or neglected. There is likely some anger, bitterness, or resentment toward God, so blaming is only going to push them further and further away with a lower chance every time of coming back.

Telling Them What They Need

This can be really tough for both sides of the equation. You assume that you know what they need, even though you are looking from the outside. You may be able to see what they need, but you have to be ready to accept that they may not want to hear it from you. Also, what you think they need may be what you want them to need and is not always the right solution. Having an outside party to either of you is usually most helpful to be objective.

Tell Them the Solution

This piggybacks on assuming you know what they need, but goes even further by telling them what the solution is. Telling them things like, "Just pray about it," or "Just take some medication" implies that you have the solution, making them feel even weaker than they already do. If there was that easy of a solution, they likely would not be sitting where they are.

Give Ultimatums

By saying things like, "I will only be with you if you are on medication," or, "You have to go to counseling or I will leave you," you do so much more damage then you can imagine. People who are struggling are already feeling defeated and usually think you are better off without them. Saying things like this is asking for them to take on a fight they cannot handle.

Get Defensive

It's in our DNA that when someone is being mean we want to get defensive and then give them a taste of their own medicine back. When my husband is in a bad headspace, I usually get the brunt of the bad mood. My instinctual reaction is to push back, say mean things back, give him the silent treatment or worse, and my go-to is to hit back below the belt and go down to his level. Here is the problem with that—it doesn't work and actually creates more problems than you started with. Fighting with someone in a bad headspace with mental illness is extremely different from fighting with someone who does not struggle.

Take It Out on Others

I can see a direct correlation between when my husband is in a bad headspace and how I start treating people, especially my kids. I am impatient, quick to anger, easily frustrated, and end up yelling at them because I am trying so hard not to express how frustrated I am with my husband being in a bad headspace. Sometimes I need to give myself a time out and recuperate and go back in and try and separate my feelings and be aware that I am a little on edge and not take it out on those around me.

Take Away

Things to Take Away from This Chapter:

There are things we can be doing that can push someone deeper into the darkness. We looked at things not to do when having someone struggling in your life:

- Engage.
- Tell them to snap out of it.
- Compare to other situations, especially worse off ones.
- Get frustrated because it is all about them.
- Push them too much and too hard.
- Tell them they are doing it for attention.
- Give in to them if they are pushing for a reaction.
- Compare their situation to yourself.
- Label them.
- Blame their relationship with God.
- Tell them what they need.
- Tell them the solution.
- Give ultimatums.
- Get defensive.
- Take it out on others.

Chapter 25: Don't Give Up

D o not give up. This is literally the most important thing I can tell you. You are their partner, their supporter, and you need to be that to them regardless of the situation. Yes, it's hard; yes, its exhausting, but don't you dare let the enemy win because you are letting your "feelings" determine the outcome of the situation. I told myself a long time ago that I would not make any major decisions in a dark time or season. Usually once you are out of the thick of it you will be able to see things more clearly and you will see the hope and the plan, and this will give you the motivation to keep on trucking along. The Bible encourages us over and over not to give up, to lean on God during times of trouble, and that as long as we follow Him in the darkness we will come out on the other side stronger and rewarded.

> Let us not become weary in doing good, for at the proper time we will reap a harvest if we do not give up (Galatians 6:9).

> But as for you, be strong and do not give up, for your work will be rewarded (2 Chronicles 15:7).

If you are the supporter in a relationship or know someone who is, I hope these ideas and advice can be helpful. It can be very scary and defeating at times trying to support someone who is struggling, and the resources are not as easy to come by, so I encourage you to reach out if you are stuck. The enemy loves to attack you in the silence, so speak up if you are in a situation where you feel stuck. You are not alone; there are solutions and ways to get out of the darkness.

Many times when someone struggling, although it looks like the contrary, they are crying out for help. After our entire situation, my husband reflected on it all and told me that when he fell into the darkness and backlashed at me it was a cry for help. I know it looks like the complete opposite. How can pushing you away and putting up barriers be a cry for help? I know it doesn't look like it, but most of the time it is. Not giving up comes back to everything we looked at with unconditional love, being committed to the relationship you have, knowing that deep down there is a good person who is hurting and struggling, and not walking away when things get hard.

> Have I not commanded you? Be strong and courageous. Do not be afraid; do not be discouraged, for the Lord your God will be with you wherever you go (Joshua 1:9).

> So do not fear, for I am with you; do not be dismayed, for I am your God. I will strengthen you and help you; I will uphold you with my righteous right hand (Isaiah 41:10).

I know in this book I talked a lot about the pain and darkness that we endured. There is also a victorious side to the story that I share as well. Watching restoration occur after fighting a battle is the most glorious feeling you will ever experience. Like you read in our story, we like to compare it to how an avalanche occurs when the snow exceeds its strength. We both had been trying to do it on our own strength for far too long. The best part of the whole story is the rescue hero who comes down to save us is not just a trained technician in avalanches, but the Creator of the entire universe! Our story is a testimony that His love prevails, conquers anything the enemy tries to use against you, and that God is victorious and triumphant when we come to Him to help us fight. There are lots of really amazing moments to being a part of God's miracle stories. In the process of restoration there are pivotal moments. One of them for us came before we moved to the town we currently live in. Our pastor asked us to speak to our church as we moved on to a new chapter of our lives and to share our testimony of what God has done. It was a moment I will never forget—watching my husband publicly acknowledge the problems he had experienced and give the glory to God for how it has changed and gotten better. Not only was it growth in his own spiritual walk, but as a by-product it strengthened our marriage.

I like to always come back to God's truth, so let's take a look at what God says about restoration.

> "But I will restore you to health and heal your wounds," declares the Lord, "because you are called an outcast, Zion for whom no one cares" (Jeremiah 30:17).

> Restore to me the joy of your salvation and grant me a willing spirit, to sustain me (Psalms 51:12).

Watching my husband talk about this was such an amazing feeling for me and hopefully for everyone who was praying for him in the battle. Like I said, this process of realizing, recognizing, and acknowledging has caused a re-ignition of strength in our marriage. When we first met, our main connection was being one of the only two Christians at a non-Christian camp. God was the factor that brought us together. If I look back even now at our years together, I see the times we were closest was when God was at work.

When we were first married, we went to a pretty life-changing Christian conference. It was a weekend where we were able to pour into our relationship with God individually and as a newly married couple. After pouring into God together, it seemed like we fell in love all over again. I feel like the struggle we just experienced that I have shared in this book, has brought us even closer again. As we as a family have hungered for God, our marriage has been strengthened, and our love has been able to go to a deeper level than we have ever experienced. I urge you to think of times this has happened in your marriage or relationship and find what the root cause of it was. Strive for this—it keeps your marriage alive!

To anyone who is going through a storm of your own: Don't give up hope! Don't allow the enemy to keep you in the darkness where he feels he has power and control; don't accept that the storm is the end—the storm is not the end. Sometimes we have to go through hard stuff to get all the brokenness chiseled away. Yet God is good, always. We don't have to go through storms alone; it is strength to lean on our brothers and sisters, not weakness like the world teaches us. God always has a beautiful plan.

Take Away

Things to Take Away from This Chapter:

- Do not give up!
- God is always the triumphant victor when we allow Him to take control of the situation.
- Restoration is the end goal and the most splendid feeling after a battle.
- Don't put limits or boundaries on what God can do and how much He can help. What we may view as impossible is very possible to God.

Conclusion

Like any story we have heard since we were young, we want stories to have a happy ending. Sadly, life does not always work that way. God performed miracles in our lives; He truly did heal. But I want to be very clear when I say that the key to understanding mental illness is accepting that it is not the flu, that it doesn't just go away after a while. There are many cases where people are healed and they do not struggle anymore. Mental illness is much trickier; it is something that, in most cases, will always be there to some degree.

In our story, God rebuilt us, God performed miracles, God gave me a new and renewed husband, but I want to be very real when I tell you that there is an aspect of mental illness that we will have to deal with forever. In our situation my husband got the help he needed and I feel like I have a new husband. But that does not mean we don't have dark hours, days, or weeks. What I have learned is that there is a threshold where the medication and coping skills that have come into our situation can help. Once we cross that threshold, there are a lot of default mindsets that he falls back into that he lived with for over a decade. It takes conscious learning and training to get out of those ingrained ways. Many people struggling with mental illness will be in similar boats. We have times when the memories of how we used to live become so real that I get terrified thinking we are going back there. God has been so good to remind me each and every time that He was victorious in the past, and in the future He is still the redeemer in each and every situation, even the dark ones. Our story is proof that He can use every single piece of a situation, every dark moment and every tear, and turn it into something

159

beautiful. The reason I say this is because I do not want you to think everything is perfect now and that because your situation is still not completely healed we are different from anyone else struggling on either side of mental illness. This is not a fairy tale but real life, and real life has sin in it and we still battle mental illness to some degree, but we are finally in a place where we can walk through it educated, courageous, and trusting that God has got this, even if it feels like we are alone.

Something remarkable I can say with certainty is that this had to happen the exact way it did. It had to get that bad and that dark for us to both hit rock bottom and only be able to look up toward God. I know now that God had a plan and that the darkness of the situation was and had to be part of that plan. The reason we are sharing our story so openly and in such detail is to encourage people on both sides of the equation. As a spouse, I am sure I made lots of wrong choices and added things to the situation that were not right. As the person struggling, my husband pushed back so hard for so many years when we potentially could have gotten this same type of help years earlier. We know that we are not the only ones in this situation—a spouse watching their spouse struggle and not knowing what to do, and a person struggling but being resistant to any type of help. This is why we are sharing our story and why I wrote this book. I want to encourage anyone in a storm to remember God is good, God has a plan, God will walk you through and out of this storm in His timing. I hope you are able to walk away with some tangible advice for how to walk the journey of supporting without enabling, to be loving, and to lay down boundaries where they are needed for the well-being of everyone involved.

My goal for this book is to bring light to mental illness in the church. In the Christian world, mental illness is not something that is openly talked about and is often looked down upon. This is not the way God intended us to walk with our brothers and sisters in Christ. We are supposed to be able to lean on each other, walk through tough times together, and not hide things or feel shameful that we are not perfect. I believe the more we bring mental illness to the light, the more we can grow as a global church and show the world that even though we face the same problems, we have something different—Jesus. Christians face the same problems as non-Christians, yet the non-Christian world is actually becoming better at speaking out and advocating about mental illness. This needs to change; I can only hope this becomes a movement and that we can start the conversation about mental illness within our churches and Christian circles. People who struggle are not weak, and mental illness is not the only thing that defines them. They are people like you and I, and we need to start changing our perspective on how we view and treat people who are struggling. I also wrote this book to reach out to the people who live on the other side of mental illness—the supporters, the ones who face an entirely different struggle that is even more silent. We need to stand strong while we live on this earth and follow the principals Jesus taught us and walk through it and trust that God will hold us the entire way.

I hope that as you have journeyed through this book with me you have a better understanding of the enemy's goals and how real the battle truly is. I hope you gained a better understanding of the mind-frame of someone struggling. I hope you found some encouragement as you support someone in your life with mental illness and learned some tangible ways you can be supportive and also take care of yourself in this role. Lastly, I hope this can start the conversation in the Christian world—that yes, of course there is a spiritual side to it, but that there are ways we can deal with it here on earth as well.

About the Author

For years, Danielle Foisy worked in the secular workplace until God asked her to take a leap of faith and leave her career to start following God's plan for her life. In the darkest and hardest times while living with a husband who struggles with mental illness, she found there were not a lot of resources for the person who is supporting someone who is struggling. The goal of this book is to change that and start the conversation.

She found writing to be a healthy coping mechanism to deal with the stress that comes with the role, and now she is using this book to help others who are in the same role she is in.

Danielle lives in Haliburton, Ontario with her husband, two young daughters, and a puppy. Outside of writing, she enjoys adventures like ice climbing, rock climbing, and other adventurous sports.

Danielle can be contacted at:

theothersideofthestruggle@gmail.com

www.daniellefoisy.com

We are a Christian-based publishing company that was founded in 2009. Our primary focus has been to establish authors.

"5 Fold Media was the launching partner that I needed to bring *The Transformed Life* into reality. This team worked diligently and with integrity to help me bring my words and vision into manifestation through a book that I am proud of and continues to help people and churches around the world. None of this would have been possible without the partnership and education I received from 5 Fold Media."

- Pastor John Carter, Lead Pastor of Abundant Life Christian Center, Syracuse, NY, Author and Fox News Contributor

*The Transformed Life is foreworded by Pastor A.R. Bernard, received endorsements from best-selling authors Phil Cooke, Rick Renner, and Tony Cooke, and has been featured on television shows such as TBN and local networks.

5 Fold Media

315.570.3333 | 5701 E. Circle Dr. #338, Cicero, NY 13039
manuscript@5foldmedia.com

Find us on Facebook, Twitter, and YouTube

Discover more at www.5FoldMedia.com.

Capturing the Supernatural

Are you ready to experience healing right here, right now?

Most of us believe (or want to believe) that God still shows up in miraculous ways—that He supernaturally intervenes in our lives. But how come it always seems to happen to someone else, often in some far-away place? This book will uplift and inspire you to believe not only that divine healing happens today, but that it's happening far more often than you might imagine.

As you read these well-documented stories of supernatural healing you will find your faith growing. Along the way you will gain fresh insight and instruction on key principles that may play a role in you receiving your healing.

> "My heart was refreshed and my spirit was stirred as I read *Healed!: Present Day Stories of Healing and How it Happens*, by my dear friends Andy and Cathy Sanders. This is a timely message for the bride of Christ! I believe that the reader will not only experience God's healing power, but they will also find that they are living at a new level of faith. This book truly captures the supernatural. It's destined to be a classic!"

— Patrick Schatzline, Founder of Remnant Ministries International
Author of *Why Is God So Mad at Me?*; *I Am Remnant*; and *Unqualified: Where You Can Begin to be Great*. www.iamremnant.me

Get ready to be encouraged and blessed as you read these candid, unfiltered accounts of supernatural healings.

Visit www.capturingthesupernatural.com for more information.

CPSIA information can be obtained
at www.ICGtesting.com
Printed in the USA
LVOW03s0856310817
547042LV00003B/4/P